Predication and Genesis

New Perspectives in Ontology
Series Editors: Peter Gratton, Southeastern Louisiana University, and Sean J. McGrath, Memorial University of Newfoundland, Canada

Publishes the best new work on the question of being and the history of metaphysics

After the linguistic and structuralist turn of the twentieth century, a renaissance in metaphysics and ontology is occurring. Following in the wake of speculative realism and new materialism, this series aims to build on this renewed interest in perennial metaphysical questions, while opening up avenues of investigation long assumed to be closed. Working within the Continental tradition without being confined by it, the books in this series will move beyond the linguistic turn and rethink the oldest questions in a contemporary context. They will challenge old prejudices while drawing upon the speculative turn in post-Heideggerian ontology, the philosophy of nature and the philosophy of religion.

Editorial Advisory Board
Maurizio Ferraris, Paul Franks, Iain Hamilton Grant, Garth Green, Adrian Johnston, Catherine Malabou, Jeff Malpas, Marie-Eve Morin, Jeffrey Reid, Susan Ruddick, Michael Schulz, Hasana Sharp, Alison Stone, Peter Trawny, Uwe Voigt, Jason Wirth, Günter Zöller

Books available
The Political Theology of Schelling, Saitya Brata Das
Continental Realism and its Discontents, edited by Marie-Eve Morin
The Contingency of Necessity: Reason and God as Matters of Fact, Tyler Tritten
The Problem of Nature in Hegel's Final System, Wes Furlotte
Schelling's Naturalism: Motion, Space and the Volition of Thought, Ben Woodard
Thinking Nature: An Essay in Negative Ecology, Sean J. McGrath
Heidegger's Ontology of Events, James Bahoh
The Political Theology of Kierkegaard, Saitya Brata Das
The Schelling–Eschenmayer Controversy, 1801: Nature and Identity, Benjamin Berger and Daniel Whistler
Hölderlin's Philosophy of Nature, edited by Rochelle Tobias
Affect and Attention After Deleuze and Whitehead: Ecological Attunement, Russell J. Duvernoy
The Philosophical Foundations of the Late Schelling: The Turn to the Positive, Sean J. McGrath
Schelling's Ontology of Powers, Charlotte Alderwick
Collected Essays in Speculative Philosophy, by James Bradley and edited by Sean J. McGrath
Merleau-Ponty and Nancy on Sense and Being: At the Limits of Phenomenology, Marie-Eve Morin
Predication and Genesis: Metaphysics as Fundamental Heuristic after Schelling's The Ages of the World, Wolfram Hogrebe, translated and edited by Iain Hamilton Grant and Jason M. Wirth

www.edinburghuniversitypress.com/series/epnpio

Predication and Genesis

Metaphysics as Fundamental Heuristic after Schelling's *The Ages of the World*

WOLFRAM HOGREBE

Translated and edited by Iain Hamilton Grant and Jason M. Wirth

EDINBURGH
University Press

Edinburgh University Press is one of the leading university presses in the UK. We publish academic books and journals in our selected subject areas across the humanities and social sciences, combining cutting-edge scholarship with high editorial and production values to produce academic works of lasting importance. For more information visit our website: edinburghuniversitypress.com

English translation © Iain Hamilton Grant and Jason M. Wirth, 2024

© Suhrkamp Verlag, Frankfurt am Main 1989.
All rights reserved by and controlled through Suhrkamp Verlag Berlin.

Edinburgh University Press Ltd
13 Infirmary Street
Edinburgh EH1 1LT

Typeset in 11/13 Adobe Garamond
by Cheshire Typesetting Ltd, Cuddington, Cheshire, and
printed and bound in Great Britain

A CIP record for this book is available from the British Library

ISBN 978 1 3995 3149 8 (hardback)
ISBN 978 1 3995 3151 1 (webready PDF)
ISBN 978 1 3995 3152 8 (epub)

The right of Wolfram Hogrebe to be identified as the author of this work has been asserted in accordance with the Copyright, Designs and Patents Act 1988, and the Copyright and Related Rights Regulations 2003 (SI No. 2498).

Contents

Acknowledgements — vii
Translators' Introduction: Synthetic Mantics — ix
Iain Hamilton Grant and Jason M. Wirth
    I. The audacity of being — ix
    II. The ubiquity of creation — xii
    A readers' guide to Hogrebe's work — xix
Books by Wolfram Hogrebe — xxii
Author's Foreword to the English Edition — xxiv
Author's Foreword to the Italian Edition (2011) — xxviii

Predication and Genesis — 1

I. Foreword — 3

II. Schelling and Dante: An Introduction to Schelling's Thinking — 11
    1. *Lectura dantis* — 11
    2. The idea of a new mythology — 14
    3. The great poem about nature — 17
    4. Schelling's interest in Dante — 19
    5. Schelling's task of a poetic version of the new mythology — 21
    6. Dante as archetype for *The Ages of the World* — 24

7. The task of an argumentative reconstruction of
The Ages of the World — 28

III. Transition to a Reconstruction of *The Ages of the World*:
Metaphysics and the Theory of Predication — 36
   8. Metaphysics and the conditions of successful predication — 37
   9. Metaphysics and the adequacy conditions of predication — 42
  10. Metaphysics and the existential conditions of predication — 46
  11. Starting conditions of predication: Kant's theory of the transcendental ideal — 52
  12. Schelling's engagement with Kant's transcendental ideal — 58
  13. Towards a theory of predicative elementary particles — 63

IV. Predication and Genesis: *The Ages of the World* — 73
  14. The predication-theoretical venture of *The Ages of the World* — 75
  15. Original negation and original affirmation — 77
  16. Predicative rotation — 87
  17. From chaos to order — 92
  18. Self-organisation and unity — 97
  19. Schelling's world formula — 103
  20. Reason and madness — 109

V. Afterword — 122

Postface: The Ontology of Predication in Schelling's
The Ages of the World — 126
Markus Gabriel

Index — 142

Acknowledgements

IHG and JMW would firstly like to thank Susanne Pfeffer, currently director of the Museum für Moderne Kunst in Frankfurt am Main, whose invitations to us to present at the seminar accompanying the exhibition *Nature after Nature*, at the Fridericianum, Kassell, in 2014, also provided the lunch during which we hatched the plan for this work with Markus Gabriel, to whom we are also grateful for his essay on *The Ages of the World* published as an appendix here.

We gratefully acknowledge Rosenberg and Sellier, for permission to include our translation of Wolfram Hogrebe's foreword to the Italian edition of this work, *Predicazione e genesi* (Turin: Rosenberg and Sellier, 2012), and to Verlag Karl Alber, Freiburg and Munich, for permission to include our translation of Markus Gabriel's essay 'Die Ontologie der Prädikation in Schellings *Die Weltalter*', from *Schelling-Studien* 2 (2014), 3–20. We are also grateful to the Staatliche Kunstsammlungen Dresden for permission to reproduce the image illustrating Schelling's seal.

IHG would like to add that no one returns from the underworld laden with treasure. My thanks to Jason Wirth for reminding me that the treasure is in the making, and that making is a communitarian issuant.

JMW and IHG wish also to register the joy it has been to work with Carol Macdonald at EUP, for which we are thankful to her.

Finally, we would like to express our warmest gratitude to Wolfram Hogrebe, who generously replied to our emails and offered materials for inclusion here that greatly enhance the present volume.

Translators' Introduction: Synthetic Mantics

Iain Hamilton Grant and Jason M. Wirth

1 The audacity of being

Schelling the philosopher and metaphysics the philosophical enterprise have this in common: when Wolfram Hogrebe's remarkable 1989 study of Schelling's tremulous, faltering and unfinished masterwork *The Ages of the World* (*Die Weltalter*) appeared, both were in general disrepute. How far away Schelling's biographical philosophical epic of the universe's autogenesis, violent tumult and all, appeared from philosophy's modest tasks and shopkeeping! And metaphysics in almost all quarters evoked suspicion and disdain, as if it were an embarrassingly errant concern of a bygone era or a lurking risk over which we had to maintain an upper hand (Heidegger's *Verwindung*).

In his blurb for the 2000 translation of the third or 1815 version of *The Ages of the World*, David Farrell Krell confirmed that the insistence that Schelling's grand experiment remained critical to philosophy was scandalous. 'Those who insist that thought be brought under a rule will send this book flying across the room.' It is not that thought is free of rules, but that to reduce thought to its rules evades a more difficult and, in some sense of the word, *properly metaphysical* question: how did it come to be subject to any kind of rules? One cannot simply use the rules of thought to explain the rules of thought. 'Never fear: Schelling's text will soar on its own, free and daring and daunting', Krell reassured us.

In this sense, we could call Hogrebe's text *fearless*. It is a remarkable work, an intervention in the prevailing academic Western quarters of our very sense of what can matter as philosophy. Rather than display Schelling's most bewildering text, his most anomalous contribution to our philosophical heritage, as translatable into what we already know about philosophy and the fate of metaphysics, Hogrebe, by invention, robustly defends it against orthodoxy. Translating it into two contemporary idioms, not only but also predicate logic, and not only but also literary analysis, he demonstrates that Schelling is not external to those traditions, but rather transforms them from the ground – or perhaps from the abyss of nonsense – up. 'That something exists at all is not a physical event!'

It is not a physical event, but rather a metaphysical event. 'The whole world is, so to speak, caught in reason, but the question is: how did it get in this net?'

What does Hogrebe's recovery of Schelling's metaphysics mean for our time? On the one hand, it is a bold challenge to contemporary philosophy's penchant for micrology. 'For reducing Schelling's metaphysical speculations to a predicative-theoretical matrix pursues the systematic interests of a recovery of metaphysical problematics for our time.' Hogrebe's translation and challenge of Schelling's 'predicate logic' allows philosophy to recover its ambition and range, much as one sees in thinkers such as Whitehead, Heidegger, Deleuze, Nishida and others. 'Metaphysics spells out the structure of the singular judgment (Fa) as the structure of the world.' It does not recover this range, however, by imagining that we can go back to primary propositions that indubitably describe the world as it is. Such a world is not simply available or given to or for us, but is itself a state in possibility-space. It might, that is, just as well not be. Thinking that it does therefore entails thinking not only that (and how) it came to be, but also how it came to be that the world's being has come additionally to involve the thought or the knowing of the world's coming to be. The conditions of the 'auto-epistemic structure' therefore extend down past the past of knowing to the 'abyss of the past' from which worlds emerge.

Metaphysics is not a set of indubitable claims about a world it assumes as given. In investigating the essence of the world, it does not produce essential determinations. 'There is no essential definition. Metaphysics in the style of essential definitions, therefore a nominal metaphysics, is not possible. Essence indeed directs our efforts to name, but the nominal net income is not a representation of the essence (otherwise these contributions would be effectively infallible).' It is rather a 'fundamental heuristic', a set of exercises and philosophical practices and experiments in which, to use Deleuze's felicitous phrase, the *image of thought*, the universe in its auto-poiesis becoming self-conscious in philosophical thought, manifests. 'By this critical limitation and the establishment of metaphysics exclusively in heuristic discourse, we can nonetheless say that the object of metaphysics is the essence of the world. And the essence of the world is the enigma of the world, or "What the world keeps closed in its innermost".'

Accordingly, Schelling's metaphysics would not be rooted in evidentiary principles, substance or a rational ground, but rather in what Hogrebe dubs 'pronominal being', in itself insusceptible to any predication but a presupposition of all. 'The fascination issuing from Schelling's metaphysics is due to the circumstance that his excavating thought reaches strata in which beings are no longer rooted, but all roots decompose: it reaches an abyss for reason which is nevertheless also its presupposition, since it must precisely keep its distance from it. From this conception, there shines a modernity we have not yet reached.' In noting this, Hogrebe echoes the philosophical futurism, the demand for invention, that also prompted the first breaths of Schelling's philosophical epic of the future.

In his famous reflections on Orpheus, whose song recollects what is but not what was, in *The Space of Literature*, Maurice Blanchot turned to writing's task as the effort to bring Eurydice back from Hades by evoking her in language without beholding her or capturing her. Of course, he will fail, and every work, every effort, is in the end the fatal gaze by which pronominal being disappears, and at the ground of the work's reference 'we confront something extinguished: a work suddenly become invisible again, which is no longer there, has never been there'.[1] For Hogrebe, the pure 'Something whatever (*irgendetwas*) exists not in "a certain kind of being", but not not at all (*nicht überhaupt nicht*).'

Here and elsewhere,[2] Hogrebe refers to this strange relation as an '*orphic reference*', in which an 'explicit reference to pure positivity makes it disappear, although all oblique references (nominal identifications) are like Orpheus being followed by Eurydice. A verificatory position shatters on pure positivity. Verification here means liquidation.'

Admittedly, the claim that predicate logic and its maximally inclusive range – all that is thinkable and knowable – is genetically unthinkable without orphic reference sounds more like madness or theology. For Hogrebe it is the overcoming of the former and the presupposition of the latter. How is this to be thought?

II The ubiquity of creation

Predication and Genesis: predication first, becoming second. 'In the beginning was the word'? Is this indeed a theology, a creation story, or is the 'pre' in predication antecedent to the telling, a *fore*-telling, or a mantic episode that, as such, requires a becoming to furnish its truthmaker? What then of the conjunction? And where then does a claim come from? Wolfram Hogrebe offers many glimpses into the semantic underworld, from whence the music of a semantic Orpheus is presaged in the creaking mantle covering Persephone's domain. Yet the problem was made definitive by replacing the predicative whence with a predicative ground, the givenness of which modernity contested. Heeding Hades' injunction, the predicative Orpheus knows that looking back will reveal only an abyss.

It is often overlooked how fond Schelling was of radicalising Kant's gestures: the critique of pure or of practical reason becomes the critique of *natural* reason, for example: of naturalism, perhaps, or of reason as anthropological fact? Or of reason subject merely to the orthodoxy of its having *a* nature? Importantly for Schelling, Kant's '*Abgrund für die menschliche Vernunft*'[3] becomes the *Ungrund* of all things because the Principle of Sufficient Reason that Kant removes in order to stare into the abyss never did have *human* reason, reason, that is, as anthropological fact, as its focus, but rather the rational order identical with the order of being, or the reason of being. In the incisive work that follows, Hogrebe emphasises the resultant meaninglessness of being: since meaning is consequent upon being, its emergence issues in a meaninglessness proper to being, so that the inquiry into the ground of meaning necessarily confronts its not obtaining as the precondition to its doing so. Our attention is here drawn not to the content of the meaning of being but to the fact of its emergence and the facts this accordingly presupposes. Pre-predicative being, in other words, is just that.

If the metaphysical dimension of the problem of meaning is thus opened by Schelling's inquiry, why focus on its consequences for philosophical semantics? Hogrebe is among those who no doubt see the irony as well as the formal or functional virtue of Tarski's truth theorem: the ground and function of meaning is precisely the absurdity of equivalence between object-language and meta-language. Perhaps the artifice in Tarski's accomplishment is part of what draws Schelling's speculations into close contact with it. At any rate, Hogrebe's agenda is premised on the one hand on making sense of Schelling's contemporaneity for philosophy by introducing his articulations and problems into that philosophy; but this is not subject to the restriction that only thus will Schelling *make sense* for us (why *that* restriction? Who *are* we that require our discipline's past to be either eclipsed by its present or made present only by eliminating its differences?) The point is precisely that this speculative naturalist, this metaphysician of time, this mythologising and revelationising philosopher operates equally in the abstractions of formal semantics as in the Baroque intricacies of classical German speculation. Accordingly, summarising Schelling's inquiry into why there is meaning rather than meaninglessness, Hogrebe functionalises both of these bivalent options in a dictum as absurd as, at first sight, Tarski's is: *Sein ist Unsinn*, being is meaningless. This will necessarily be true if there are no final satisfiers of the Principle of Sufficient Reason. Yet neither does Hogrebe's formulation entail that contemporary philosophers of language should embrace their inner, long-denied metaphysician and explicate the Principle of Reason's *insufficiency*. Rather, the metaphysical dimension of the problem that Hogrebe's inquiries here engage with consists in examining reason not only by means of reason, but rather through the lens of being that precedes it, that is, *a priori* in the strict or fullest sense of the term.

Thus, like Schelling, the reason Hogrebe examines is *not only* but *also* anthropological fact, for which reason his works have repeatedly brought the basic epistemic directedness of rational inquiry into closer contact than contemporary philosophy otherwise allows with those other cognitive practices left primarily to anthropology to acknowledge: hence the titles of *Metaphysics and Divination: The Interpretive Nature of Humanity* (1992) and *Knowledge and Presentiment: Drafts of a Theory of Natural Cognition* (1996), which bring epistemology into contact with cognitive states such as foresight and anticipation, provide echoes in our contemporary philosophical caves of a Schellingianism that is *not only* but *also* a philosophical anthropology decidedly unlike its contemporary namesake. The resemblance these projects bear to Schelling's own *Philosophy of Mythology*, for example, which treats mythology not as a curious object domain for reasoning about but rather finds species of reason in it elsewhere unexemplified, does not have as its focus the recoding or interpretation of myth into other *logoi*, but rather the demonstration of the issuances of *these* modes of reason or worldmaking.

We cannot but be struck by the rational impiety of these projects, or the impiousness of a *participant rationality* (a modality of Schelling's *Mitwissenschaft*?): the invention of additional worlds rather than sheltering in the immanentist orthodoxy of the oneness of all things. As Eleatic Zeno protested, 'if anyone could make clear to him what the one is, he would be able to speak of the things that are' (DK 29 A16). Indeed, the possibility of settled unities fundamentally antithetical to makings is one of the key targets both of Hogrebe's Schelling in this volume, and of the work of Markus Gabriel, whose development of Hogrebe's Schelling postulates forms part of the present volume. It permits us to reach back to an earlier iteration of Hogrebe's method in *Kant and the Problem of a Transcendental Semantics* (1974).

Evident both in that and in the present work is the requirement – itself historical – that past knowledge be remade not only according to our own times but also in accordance with knowledge's own times, that is, in accordance with its object, the content of knowing condemned to form the unrecoverable past of that knowledge, as Schelling famously hypothesises at the outset of *The Ages of the World*. The past of a particular knowing or the knowledge of a particular something cannot, of course, be the same as the past that includes that past that contains the knowing of a past proper to that second past. Nor, self-evidently, can present knowledge of its immediate past be equivalent to the succession of pasts that knowledge presupposes, assuming simply that present knowledge does not equal past knowledge. Nor can any present or future knowledge sum those knowledges, each of which have their own pasts yet now themselves belong to a past proper to additional and subsequent knowledges. The acknowledgement, in other words, that the knowledge of a past is not equivalent to the successive pasts in which knowledge will always be made to consist demonstrates the problem of a merely inherited pastness, as opposed, for example, to the mantic or 'senti-mental' (i.e., that mentality indistinct from sense capable therefore of *discernment*, as again *The Ages of the World* notes at its outset) quasi-epistemic modalities that Hogrebe considers across several of his many works.

To follow the opening claims of *The Ages of the World*, then, it is a consequence not merely of the *critique* or myth of givenness but rather of its *history* that the so-called given is as susceptible of what Hogrebe has called an 'archaeology' as are self-evident constructs such as postulates or axioms.[4] The concept of construction, that is, neither divides 'artefact' from 'given' nor renders them equivalent, because, as all the drafts of *The Ages of the World* set out at the first, all constructions issue from histories that they neither sum nor are capable of summing. It is in this sense that knowings share with their objects the status of 'worldly outcomes', as Schelling might have put it, demonstrating the 'actuality of thinking' that Hogrebe asserts.[5] It is in this, rather than the not only but also epistemic register of Kant's question concerning the possibility of a *synthetic a priori*, that irreversibility acquires its metaphysical significance, as do Schelling's radicalisations of Kant's gestures – the historicity of knowings, if all knowing is a *participant epistemology*, will always consist in syntheses, that is, in makings rather than only their deliverances: this is not merely a fact of reason for finite beings, but a fact of any cosmos among whose children such beings number. The question is not *only* therefore of the meaning of being, but the *being* of the meaning of being, a question that is insuperably recurrent because that transcendental being is consistently remade. When therefore Schelling argues that 'being itself is nothing other than construction itself (*das Seyn selbst nichts anderes als das Construiren selbst… ist*)',[6] it is the *activity* we are to hear in the infinitives; not the spurious claim that being is a finite number of *finished* constructions, but the construct*ing* is the be*ing*.

Hence, ultimately, the coincidence of meaning and ontogeny that is among the themes of *Predication and Genesis*. Hence also, perhaps, Hogrebe's and Schelling's contrast of the epos and the Principle of Sufficient Reason is additionally a facet of a *synthetic a priori*: what the principle is premised on making ahistorically given, the epos is premised on deriving. 'Why this time, this space; why this body, these thoughts?', as Handke and Wenders might ask alongside Dante and Virgil. Such philosophical epics as Schelling, too, wished to write contrive an actuality insulated against alternatives by *making* the initial conditions leading to that actuality. This is certainly an 'impious' move:[7] all theogony is a forgery or a theopoiesis, not because the – or any – gods are simply given, but because gods appear and go under, according to the Hesiodic account, in generations. Insulation is thus provided at a cost: PSR-compliance by epos entails that there are always more odysseys, more comedies, divine or otherwise, because their domain internality, so to speak, their made world, is secured to the extent that it is local. As Zeno noted: make clear what the one is, and I'll show you the many that are. Again, therefore, the metaphysical dimension of synthetic PSR satisfaction is demonstrated: no ontology entailing finality of form can accommodate the ontogeny from which it issues as a discrete spacetime.

And here, too, we confront an additionally Schellingian theme: historicity, *Geschichtlichkeit*, is not brought to the end that *das Geschehenen* suggests, but is the worldly *poiesis* made sensuous by, for example, Hogrebe's transcendental reworking of semantics after Schelling: as we said earlier, the synthetic recasting of the question of the meaning of being is not only but also mythic-anthropologonic, geogonic, theogonic because ontically satisfied: there comes to be a being proper to the meaning of being. And this is due to the historicity of the making of knowing, as Ritter pointed out in *Physics as Art*: '*die Wissenschaft ist das, was das Wissen, schafft*': science is what knowing makes.[8]

At last, therefore, through these *Wissenschaftliche* prose-poems, we glimpse the philosophical whole that Schelling's thinking articulates when it speaks as clearly, truly and beautifully as does this book. What variety of instruments are deployed in the making that thinking is? This *not only but also* involves, *inter alia*, anthropological, technical, historical, poietic, divinatory and theogonic questions to which, in their reciprocally divergent registers, both Schelling and Hogrebe respond in similarly plural ways. It raises in turn a question concerning what might be called the 'futuribility' of the transcendental philosophy that is among the greatest of modernity's inventions. Transcendental philosophy is certainly too narrowly conceived as the thinking that reflects on its own operations, for this conception neglects the sheer variety of instruments that our question suggests are available in philosophy's unsatisfied organon. Indeed, that it has one or only one such instrument – call it 'reason' – is contested by the mere fact of the discipline of the history of philosophy.

Perhaps this raises the suspicion that, for all its reworking, it is in the end only or merely the history of philosophy to which the present work contributes. Schelling, after all, is no contemporary of ours, but a superseded historical relay between Kant and Hegel, forgotten by all but specialist scholars of the period. Yet this is to treat history as equivalent only to the totality of *das Geschehenen*, of what *has happened*, or as the totality of what *is to be known*. Such a history is not, of course, the history of *philosophy* or, better, the *historicising* that philosophy must perform if it can, and that therefore must be remade to accommodate new inventions or 'progress', depending on our point of view. The philosopher is a node in what has happened, and thus among the finished facts of such a history, but her philosophy itself may not yet have 'happened' or *be happening* – in the sense that a specific cultural trajectory may be said to be 'happening'. In this sense, as Hogrebe here shows, though Schelling is not our contemporary, Schellingianisms are – and perhaps will also turn out to be the historicising truthmaker of Jaspers' claim that Schelling had, by the mid-twentieth century, produced no school or movement.[9]

Likewise, Schelling too practises *inter alia* a species of transcendental philosophy, albeit one subject, as we noted earlier, to his radicalisations. But this accompanies, as he repeatedly states, the *Naturphilosophie* alongside it, and which therefore is no mere *continuation* of it, nota bene. To these will be added in time a philosophy of mythology and of revelation, though at the core of the whole is the great project of philosophical-historical epochality he pursues via anthropology, poietics and metaphysics in *The Ages of the World*. This is simultaneously a fact of Schelling's philosophical instruments, and of the historicity of philosophy, and gives sense to the *Mitwissenschaft* he addresses in the last-named work, which receives so probative an examination in the work to follow. A *Mitwissenschaft* by definition can have no single instrument or object as its satisfier, no matter how small (microfundamentalism) or large (monocosmism).

Operating in accordance with this innovatory organon – perhaps this clarifies one aspect of the mysterious conjunction of mythology and technology in Hogrebe's frontispiece of the Sphinx with the wheel of Nemesis in Schelling's seal – transcendental philosophy is, then, no mere reflection on *its* method but incorporates the production of instruments of thought transformatively into what will *next* count as thought. Transcendental philosophy is, in the sense in which Hogrebe's experiments below demonstrate, a philosophical surrealism, to cite the title of his recent work, of bizarre conjunctions.[10] In this same vein (are such words permissible in a time of vaccines?), why do we standardly not consider prophecy and presentiment as epistemic instruments and objects while worrying about uniformity and natural law as Humeans do, or about the projectability of predicates as Goodman does? Plutarch and Damascius could as happily accommodate both in their times as Schelling, thanks to Hogrebe's work, now can in ours. Perhaps if philosophical surrealism emphasises the conjunction, a similarly philosophical suprematism would additionally emphasise the next fold in which reason will operate, a conjunctive mantics or, again, a *Mitwissenschaft*. As Ritter reminds us, co-making is what all science (all philosophy) does; to call this 'historical' is almost therefore an empty repetition of terms, if the synthetic is always and therefore still *a priori*. What seems to be merely something that has happened, something of the past and therefore something at least knowable, only was what it was by virtue of a past that is now another object entirely. The transcendental or 'suprematicist' function of historicity is that remaking is no impious betrayal of an integral past but the only possibly adequate response to the unsettling fact of a synthesis prior to all being. Poiesis, that is, is primary, such that creation is ubiquitous. Eurydice's petrified afterlife is a fact, but incomplete without exploiting her capacity for remaking.

And thus, we are used in historical philosophy to the dead coming back to life.

A readers' guide to Hogrebe's work

As a brief orientation for the many philosophers for whom this might be their first encounter with Wolfram Hogrebe's thought, it is worth considering his first book, entitled *Kant and the Problem of Transcendental Semantics* (*Kant und das Problem einer transzendentaler Semantik*, 1974), as setting out a strategic agenda, the implications of which his subsequent work has elaborated and extended. While the classical German philosophers – Kant, Fichte, Schelling and Hegel – supply his ongoing work with pivotal reimaginings of philosophy as insuperably transcendental (his 2022 collection *Ligatures* contains a recent Schelling essay and opens with one on Novalis), then much like post-Sellarsian appropriations of Hegel's thought, he subjects these classical German philosophers to further reimaginings through the essential disciplines of contemporary philosophy: logic, epistemology, semantics and hermeneutics. Nor, however, do such disciplines survive this present encounter unaltered. In *Metaphysics and Mantics* (*Metaphysik und Mantik*, 1992; 2nd edn, 2013), for example, Hogrebe opens epistemology to cognate yet contrary practices of inquiry such as divination, as *Intuition and Cognition* (*Ahnung und Erkenntnis*, 1996) investigates the epistemic pertinence of feeling to a general heuristics (in contrast to the epistemic critique of 'raw feels' so crucial to later twentieth-century epistemology). That students of Schelling's *The Ages of the World* might recognise variants of both 'divination' and 'sensed discernment' from that work's opening pages further alerts us to the complex interweaving of philosophical resources that Hogrebe's work accomplishes.

This complexity equally extends to those formative figures of late twentieth-century French philosophy such as Derrida, for instance, to whose work Hogrebe refers from his earliest publications to his most recent (e.g. *Duplex*, 2018). Nor is his address to such material chiefly critical, as is that of his contemporary Manfred Frank (*What is Neostructuralism?*, 1989). Instead, he shares these late structuralists' enthusiasm for conceptual innovation, and in consequence negotiates his own reconceptions alongside those of Foucault (cf. *Archaeological Postulates of Meaning*, 1977) as often as alongside those of Frege, Quine or Wittgenstein. He is as critical of constructivism as is the later Wittgenstein of his own, only not on the grounds of its conceptual creativity but rather because, unlike, say, Carnap's *Aufbau*, he recognises construction as a recurrence of what the present volume calls the 'auto-epistemic structure of the world'. Self-construction, that is, is not exclusively characteristic of cognising organisms, but occurs there in consequence of its ubiquity elsewhere.

The systematic character of this echo structure for Hogrebe's philosophy is evident in turn in what *Metaphysics and Mantics* calls 'indiscrete ontology'. An ontology is indiscrete when, like William Blake, it acknowledges outlines not as final but as local. In other words, the domain of discrete beings is parasitic upon ontological indiscretion. It is in consequence of this that Hogrebe's work seeks to explore what he simply calls the 'semantic underworld', or a modernist philosophical eternity in which mythology, as the philosophers of the early nineteenth century required, becomes again inseparable from science. In accomplishing this reintegration, Hogrebe's often breathtakingly concise writings challenge the received wisdoms of the specialisations and restrictions taken for granted in contemporary philosophy to aspire again to that practice's properly non-specific range.

Notes

1. Maurice Blanchot, *The Space of Literature*, trans. Ann Smock (Lincoln, NE: University of Nebraska Press, 1982), 174.
2. See, for example, Hogrebe's account of his own 'Orphic System' as presented in his *Metaphysik und Mantik. Die Deutungsnatur des Menschen* [*Metaphysics and Mantics. The Interpretive Nature of Humanity*] (Frankfurt: Suhrkamp, 1992), 9.
3. *Critique of Pure Reason*, trans. Paul Guyer and Allen W. Wood (Cambridge: Cambridge University Press, 1998), hereafter *CPR*, A613/B641.
4. Wolfram Hogrebe, *Archäologische Bedeutungspostulate* [*The Archaeological Postulates of Meaning*] (Munich: Alber, 1977).
5. Wolfram Hogrebe, *Die Wirklichkeit des Denkens* [*The Actuality of Thought*] (Heidelberg: Winter, 2007).
6. SW I/3, 12, trans. Keith R. Peterson, *First Outline of a System of the Philosophy of Nature* (Albany, NY: State University of New York Press, 2004), hereafter *First Outline*, 13.

7. On 'impiety', see Plato, *Euthyphro* 3b: 'he says I am a godmaker…'
8. Jocelyn Holland (ed. and trans.), *Key Texts of Johann Wilhelm Ritter (1776–1810) on the Science and Art of Nature* (Leiden: Brill, 2010), 536–7.
9. Karl Jaspers, *Schelling. Größe und Verhängnis* (Munich: Piper, 1955), 213.
10. Wolfram Hogrebe, *Philosophischer Surrealismus* [*Philosophical Surrealism*] (Berlin: Akademie, 2014).

Books by Wolfram Hogrebe

Ligaturen [*Ligatures*] (Frankfurt: Klostermann, 2022)
Das Zwischenreich [*The Interworld*] (Frankfurt: Klostermann, 2020)
Szenische Metaphysik [*Scenic Metaphysics*] (Frankfurt: Klostermann, 2019)
Duplex [*Duplex*] (Frankfurt: Klostermann, 2018)
Metaphysische Einflüsterungen [*Metaphysical Insinuations*] (Frankfurt: Klostermann, 2017)
Das neue Bedürfnis nach Metaphysik [*The New Want of Metaphysics*] (ed., with Markus Gabriel; Berlin: Walter de Gruyter, 2015)
Philosophischer Surrealismus [*Philosophical Surrealism*] (Berlin: Akademie, 2014)
Der implizite Mensch [*The Implicit Human Being*] (Berlin: Akademie, 2013)
Metaphysik und Mantik [*Metaphysics and Mantik*] (2nd edn; Berlin: Akademie, 2013; Frankfurt: Suhrkamp, 1992)
Beuysianismus [*Beuysianism*] (Munich: Fink, 2011)
Riskante Lebensnähe: die szenische Existenz der Menschen [*Dangerously Close to Life: The Scenic Existence of Human Beings*] (Berlin: Akademie, 2009)
Die Wirklichkeit des Denkens [*The Actuality of Thought*] (Heidelberg: Winter, 2007)
*Phänomen und Analyse: Grundbegriffe der Philosophie der 20.Jahrhunderts in Erinnerung an Hegels Phänomenologie des

Geistes [*Phenomenon and Analysis: Basic Concepts of Twentieth-Century Philosophy in Memory of Hegel's Phenomenology of Spirit*] (ed.; Würzburg: Königshausen and Neumann, 2007)
Echo des Nichtwissens [*Echo of Unknowing*] (Berlin: Akademie, 2006)
Mantik. Profile prognostischen Wissens in Wissenschaft und Kultur [*Mantics. Profiles of Prognostic Cognition in Science and Culture*] (ed.; Würzburg: Königshausen and Neumann, 2005)
Jakob Friedrich Fries (ed., with Kay Hermann; Berlin: Peter Lang, 1999)
Subjektivität [*Subjectivity*] (ed.) (Berlin: Akademie, 1998)
Ahnung und Erkenntnis [*Intuition and Cognition*] (Frankfurt: Suhrkamp, 1996)
Fichtes Wissenschaftslehre 1794 (ed.; Frankfurt: Suhrkamp, 1995)
Prädikation und Genesis (Frankfurt: Suhrkamp, 1989)
Deutsche Philosophie im XIX. Jahrhundert [*German Philosophy in the Nineteenth Century*] (Munich: Fink, 1987)
Archäologische Bedeutungspostulate [*The Archaeological Postulates of Meaning*] (Freiburg/Munich: Alber, 1977)
Kant und das Problem einer transzendentaler Semantik [*Kant and the Problem of Transcendental Semantics*] (Freiburg/Munich: Alber, 1974)

Foreword to the English Edition

Schelling's *The Ages of the World* remains provocative in our own times. Inspired by predicate logic, my 1989 reconstruction of this remarkable book sets out from the fact that it has to do with an analysis of a structure of formative process that has universal significance. What Schelling attempts here is to expose a pattern of self-discovery, a structure invariant for ontological, cosmological, psychological and theological discourse. This is admittedly an ambitious goal. I, in any case, remain convinced that this was exactly Schelling's intuition, even if we would certainly have to define and work out the project more clearly.

The fundamental difficulty for understanding *The Ages of the World* is its attempt to develop a structure in which we are all incorporated, but which, as a living structure, is at the same time not something capable of objectification. We would have to say that it permeates us. Schelling wants to write a biography that is simultaneously our own and that of God and the World. We are familiar with this undertaking from Plato's *Timaeus*. Schelling was certainly thinking of this text, but his ambition went much farther. He also wanted to integrate the self-birthing of God into this biography. In Plato's model, this is only the case retrospectively, so to speak, and not actually genetically developed. This, in any case, was Schelling's concern, and precisely this ambition lent his project a breadth that can hardly be overstated. A complete biography of this kind has nothing outside itself, where what becomes is each a self, that is to say, all.

Research on this has prompted reflection on how it is that Schelling only properly worked out *The Past*, which would thus abandon the tripartite structure he adopted from taking Dante's *Divina commedia* as a guide. I am nowadays no longer so certain that an anamnetically recovered past cannot be entirely complete, containing the present and the future with it, so far as this can be justified philosophically. In that case, the present model of *The Ages of the World* would need no further supplementation at all. Schelling must have ruminated long on this, but it explains why, at any rate, no present or future was forthcoming. Indeed, the past also always remains a present and hence also something futural. Only specific accentuations are required, to which Schelling had obviously no access.

A final thesis such as this naturally presupposes that the manuscripts lost in the Second World War[1] contained nothing further concerning *The Ages of the World*. To this extent, we will probably never know whether Schelling in fact grappled with such an end for *The Ages of the World*.

Technically then, *The Ages of the World* is concerned to set up a structure susceptible of biography. It must therefore consider an individual structure that is onto-creative. Therefore, such a structure cannot *a limine* be justified syntactically. We may certainly say, trivially:

Everything is $(\forall x)(\exists y)(x = y)$

But if we want to say:

There is at most one $(\exists y)(\forall x)(x = y)$,

then this is simply false. However, according to Schelling, we need both together, but this is not possible syntactically. For this reason, he chose a dynamic structure for which the organism served as a model. This singular structure must contain everything within it, yet not all at once, but rather evolutionarily. The problem is simply that this structure must also generate itself. Only if it does precisely this will everything else be generated. Moreover, this self-generating structure generates itself from prerequisites that are not in its power and that are never wholly resolved into it. We are therefore dealing with an internal duality within a self-generating structure, whose obscure part is the abyss within the *space of reasons*, which is what has given *The Ages of the World*'s project its exceeding charm. Here at the latest the reader will become vertiginous to the point of bewilderment. But it is only thus that Schelling manages to integrate not only ontology, but also the entirety of psychology and theology into this simultaneously anamnetic and projective structure. Even our clearest self-consciousness in fact lives off prerequisites that are not in its power. And the same goes for God. According to Schelling's design, he himself equally lives off prerequisites that cannot be resolved without remainder into him. Schelling's conception is monistic, but it operates with a cryptic dualism in the One in order to be able to think its dynamics. Such a self-generating structure is in any case, according to Schelling's model, at the same time the structure of everything, excepting what remains without structure in an epistemic black hole.

Now whether *The Ages of the World* has met this demand, every generation of readers must decide for themselves. On my interpretation, however, it is sufficient that such a project be tackled at all. For before Schelling, no one had devised such a structure. In many contemporary philosophers, one can moreover gain the positive impression that, in a modified form, they are working on the explication of such a structure. Yet most do not know that this idea stems from Schelling.[2]

In fact, the conventional compass in which philosophical problems are nowadays formulated would appear somewhat impoverished to him. According to him, philosophy should have to do with the whole, otherwise we do not need it, not in any case as a dry-cleaning firm for arguments without metaphysical bite. In one passage, he once remarked: 'Scientific philosophy can only be speculative, but the speculative consists in contemplating the possible.'[3]

Philosophy is largely missing the *contemplative* virtue of the possible. Perhaps we may at least in this respect still learn something today from Schelling's sensibility.

Wolfram Hogrebe

Notes

1. [As the editor of the typescripts discovered in the vaults of the library of Munich University in 1944 famously remarked, no one knows what was lost when that library was destroyed soon afterwards by the Allied bombing of that city – tr.]
2. After the masterful achievement of Jason M. Wirth's translation, *The Ages of the World* (Albany, NY: State University of New York Press, 2000), this might change.
3. F. W. J. Schelling, *Einleitung in die Philosophie* [*Introduction to Philosophy*], ed. Walter E. Ehrhardt (Stuttgart-Bad Canstatt: Frommann-Holzboog, 1989), 95. On this, see also Wolfram Hogrebe, *Philosophischer Surrealismus* [*Philosophical Surrealism*] (Berlin: Akademie, 2014), 43–58.

Foreword to the Italian Edition (2011)

During my time as a *Privatdozent* at the University of Düsseldorf, Manfred Frank, himself also a *Privatdozent* there at that time, regularly presented events on Schelling's philosophy, which I attended. Indeed, I had already been acquainted with Schelling since my schooldays, but a professional familiarisation with his thought was something else entirely. When Frank then, in 1982, took up the call to Geneva as Jeanne Herrsch's successor, Schelling vanished from the curriculum at the University of Düsseldorf. Otherwise, there was not much going on in the Schelling literature during the 1980s. In 1986, invited by the Dante Society in Krefeld, I gave a presentation on Schelling's interpretation of Dante and decided to give a lecture on *The Ages of the World* during the summer semester of 1987. This remarkable text had fascinated me from a young age.

At the beginning of 1987, two months prior to the start of the summer semester, I began my preparation and soon noted that I had taken on a somewhat abysmal burden. In any case – it worked. Under the pressure of circumstances, the book was in fact written in two months. It appeared with Suhrkamp in 1989. And then the scene exploded; one book after another on Schelling has appeared since the beginning of the 1990s. These works were certainly already emerging at the end of the 1980s, above all in the circle surrounding the work on the Munich edition, of which, however, I knew nothing.

The overriding intention of the text was an attempt to introduce Schelling's thought, with as little abridgement as possible, as being capable of a connection with modern philosophical discourse. Schelling is clearly an interlocutor for those interested in modern metaphysics, a metaphysics curving out from its non-epistemic dimension only then to be caught in predicative structures.

For Schelling, this matrix is poignant because, as many overlook, logic and metaphysics have the same basic source.[1] Naturally, this focus does not sediment all Schelling's intentions into my text, and I have expressly noted this. A fundamental structure does become visible, however, without which the entirety of his later thought could hardly be made comprehensible. Nevertheless, there also remains in Schelling's manner of thinking something close to philosophy's wish structure, as Charles Baudelaire saw it: 'as if compelled by the cry of a despairing soul'.[2]

It is precisely in this that the fascination of his thought consists. In the years since, in seminars and at the universities of Jena and then Bonn, I have always continued to attempt the most transparent possible reconstruction of his thought, while thematising other aspects.[3] Today, I would telegraph the core of Schelling's fundamental thought, following Kant, thus:

I. Kant's idea of transcendental deduction.

1) If we speak of entities, we require the identity relation (*ens et unum convertuntur*, Quine, 'no entity without identity')

If entity, then identity
(logical premise)

2) No unified it without a unified I

The identity relation cannot be had without self-identity

If identity, then self-identity
(epistemological premises)

3) When we speak of identity, there is no result without self-identity

If entity, then self-identity
(from 1 and 2)

4) Without thematising self-identity, neither can we thematise entities

If no self-consciousness, then no entities
(counterposition from 3)

Thesis (4) is Kant's basic thought, and was also accepted by German idealism. Self-identity itself cannot as such be expressed in acts of knowing (syntheses), but simply documented. It 'shows itself' in acts of synthesis. Kant therefore calls the insight into this condition 'transcendental'. More precisely: what simply 'shows' itself in our cognitive achievements as their very condition is called 'transcendental'. And the systematic study of such conditions is then something like 'transcendental philosophy'.

However, the idealists were also critical of his argument. Hence Fichte held (3) and (4) to be too weak. On this interpretation, self-identity is indeed only the necessary condition for our *talk* of entities. According to Fichte, the following must also hold:

5) *If self-identity, then entity already*
(Fichte's self-referential argument in the *Science of Knowledge*)

If we accept this augmented version, then, according to Schelling's criticism of Fichte in turn, it ought also to hold that:

6) Whoever does not thematise entities cannot thematise self-identity either; no I without nature

If not entity, nor then self-identity
(counterposition from 5: Schelling's argument from nature-philosophy)

Schelling's next development then consists in deep excavations of Fichte's not-I, in order to make the genesis of a transparent self-consciousness from it transparent in turn. Nature must at any rate emerge from itself. In Fichte, conversely, it is the I that must emerge from itself. In the *Science of Knowledge* this happens first in the form of a *longing* (*SK* § 10). In Schelling, nature only emerges from itself in the form of a longing.[4] Both think this emergence as intentionality, that of the I for Fichte, that of nature for Schelling.

Who is correct? Hegel's answer: both at once. Schelling is correct because without nature's 'backing' we could make nothing realistically comprehensible. Fichte is correct because as intentional beings we have an unsaturated, and thus a projective and constructive position in the world. Yet, according to Hegel, both are mistaken in that they cannot grasp the thought of a cohesiveness of their basic positions. To this extent, they only terminate in Hegel's 'leveraged' final structure, as 'absolute liberation'.[5]

The later Schelling would certainly retort: this final structure remains insufficient. It mistakes on its part that it is only possible from prerequisites that it never entirely resolves, or even should not be resolved into it, because otherwise it would immediately collapse. 'Absolute liberation', that is, complete self-transparency, is impossible. There is only knowledge on the presupposition of non-knowledge, which could not be made epistemically transparent.

Again, then, who is correct, Hegel or the later Schelling? I conjecture Schelling. It says something genuine about it that our questioning constitution only exists because we ourselves and, ultimately, the world as a whole, remain opaque to us. And if there was no questioning constitution, we would not exist as thinking beings. A person is that which in us merely seeks itself as a person. In themselves, humans are 'search engines'. We are in ourselves something given in our seeking ourselves. Schelling's philosophy is universal heuristics.

How fruitful this is for contemporary thinking has been confirmed for some time, above all by Markus Gabriel's work.[6] In his last book in particular, *Transcendental Ontology*,[7] he modelled the design of a new ontological question framework on the madness of Schelling's thought, that we should never forget, in all our constructive successes, that we think *a parte rei*.[8] Thinking is also a form of being, and to acknowledge this is a higher kind of humility.

Interestingly, precisely this insight of Goethe's was left immune to Schiller's idealistic attitudes. In his letter to Schiller of 9 July 1796 from Weimar, Goethe is possibly speaking in the mocking, or at least ironic, manner of a *dissimulatio honesta sui*, of 'a certain realist tic' proper to him, even stemming from the 'depths of [his] nature'. He asks Schiller immediately to comment, in case he,

Goethe, did not manage to formulate this realistic option. For its content is that which he, 'from the strangest tyranny of nature', is 'incapable of uttering'.

Schiller wrote back to him in Weimar on 9 November 1796 and immediately conceded: 'You must ... never deny what you call your realist tic.'[9] What Goethe is concerned with, however, is something we could not deny. It is the uninterpreted realist option as such, from which we could not exit, since only this makes validity relations possible for us at all, that is, the true/false distinction. That this realist option is first given only in the form of a realist feeling, as the feeling of being, is not in any way contrary to its facticity, for we can only experience any facticity by way of this 'tic' or feeling. In fact, we can only be deceived about this basis if we are intoxicated by pride in our abilities. All the Swabian thinkers who in their time came to Jena – Schelling, Hegel, Hölderlin – were convinced by this insight. On the basis of this conviction they took against Fichte. And Markus Gabriel, too, has modelled his transcendental ontology project on this fundamental, realist position.

This twist in thinking, as can be seen here *a parte rei*, is not a thinker's or a poet's *idée fixe*, but rather the reversion to an anthropological fact that, notoriously, was ignored by systems theories and constructivisms of all shades. Contemporarily, Horst Bredekamp's theory of the image-act is also conceived from this turn.[10] No wonder that the reader contaminated by constructivism has difficulties with it. The ground to which all self-understanding is owed is not our act, but always already precedes our doing. We are only capable of our own acts as a dimension of the presupposition of an impotence, which is projected into us as dimension of anonymity. Here, too, there is much to think about.

Wolfram Hogrebe

Notes

1. See F. W. J. Schelling, *Zur Geschichte der neueren Philosophie*, SW I/10, 62 [trans. Andrew Bowie as *On the History of Modern Philosophy* (Cambridge: Cambridge University Press, 1994), p. 86: 'the formal-logical differentiation of thought, judgment and inference, and the material differentiation of the metaphysical concepts flow from one and the same source.' – tr.].

2. Charles Baudelaire, 'The Pagan School' (1852), in Lois Boe Hyslop and Francis E. Hyslop (trans. and ed.), *Baudelaire as Literary Critic* (University Park, PA: University of Pennsylvania Press, 1964), 75.
3. See Wolfram Hogrebe, *Echo des Nichtwissens* [*Echo of Unknowing*] (Berlin: Akademie, 2006), section IV, 'Schellingiana: Malheur de l'existence', 277–344.
4. On this, see Wolfram Hogrebe, 'Sehnsucht und Erkenntnis [Longing and Knowledge]', in *Echo des Nichtwissens*, ch. II.7, 125ff.
5. G. W. F. Hegel, *Science of Logic*, trans. A. V. Miller (London: George Allen and Unwin, 1969), 843.
6. See Markus Gabriel, *Das Absolute und die Welt in Schellings Freiheitsschrift* [*The Absolute and the World in Schelling's Freedom Essay*] (Bonn: Bonn University Press, 2006); *Der Mensch im Mythos. Untersuchungen über Ontotheologie, Anthropologie und Selbstbewußtseinsgeschichte in Schellings 'Philosophie der Mythologie'* [*Man in Myth. Investigations into Ontotheology, Anthropology, and the History of Self-Consciousness in Schelling's Philosophy of Mythology*] (Berlin: Springer, 2006); and with Slavoj Žižek, *Mythology, Madness and Laughter: Subjectivity in German Idealism* (London: Coninuum, 2009).
7. Markus Gabriel, *Transcendental Ontology. Essays in German Idealism* (London: Bloomsbury, 2011).
8. See ibid., 156 n.96: 'Schelling goes on to ask the crucial question of how the thing itself comes to appear, that is, how unprethinkable being makes its way into the dimension of sense. This question asks how the thing itself departs from itself and enters into thought: hereby, Schelling seeks to explain the *phenomenalisation* of the thing in thinking.'
9. Both letters are found in the [*Sämtliche Werke*] *Münchener Ausgabe*, ed. Manfred Beetz and Karl Richter, vol. 8.1: *Briefwechsel zwischen Schiller und Goethe in den Jahren 1794–1805* (Munich: Hanser, 1990), 208–9, 211 n.12. Ingo Meyer relativises Goethe's vocation to his realistic tic determined as the source of a misunderstanding rich in consequences, in *Im Banne der Wirklichkeit? Studien zum Problem des deutschen Realismus und seinen narrative-symbolistischen Strategien* [*Under the Spell of Actuality? Studies on the Problem of German Realism and its Narrative-Symbolist Strategies*] (Würzburg: Könnigshausen and Neumann, 2009), 193. Meyer is certainly correct with reference to the so-called 'realism' of Goethe's *Wilhelm Meister*. Read as a philosophical option, we must certainly take Goethe's remark seriously. On this, see Rüdiger Safranski's sensitive interpretation in *Goethe und Schiller. Geschichte einer Freundschaft* [*Goethe and Schiller. The History of a Friendship*] (Munich: Hanser, 2009), 136–7, 208.
10. See Horst Bredekamp, *Theorie des Bildakts* [*Theory of the Image-Act*] (Frankfurt: Suhrkamp, 2010).

Figure I.1 Schelling's Insignia, 'Greek Sphinx with Nemesis' Wheel'[1]
Image © Staatliche Kunstsammlungen Dresden

1. Schelling describes his insignia in the opening lines of his poem 'An die Geliebte' (24 December 1812): 'The sphinx has long lain, calmly stretched, at the head of intimate letters, as once before the temple. Now the letters are opened, and everyone reads the secret…' To these lines, K. F. A. Schelling adds the following footnote, which erroneously refers to the right rather than the left paw: 'The insignia that Schelling used shows a sphinx holding her right paw over a wheel' (SW X, 451).

1
Foreword

It speaks (of) wisdom, if a beginning must already have been made, to make an ironic start:

> 'Deep is the well of the past. Should we not call it bottomless?'[1]

Even though it's abysmal, the poet begins with laughter. And the beginning is all the easier, since the spirit of storytelling has already anticipated it. What does it need the poet for? – The bells are already ringing.[2] In the midst of what has happened, a beginning, then, has already been made. Again and again, *a conditional beginning*, certainly. But the historian, the poet, find nothing else in the past. And politicians are grateful: even beginnings such as these – *Ab urbe condita* (Livy)[3] or *usque ad urbem conditam* (Virgil)[4] – are primal events where memory 'may find national reassurance … and come to historical and personal rest'.[5] Concerning these *conditional kinds of origins*, the poet is well aware 'that the well's depths can in no way be considered earnestly plumbed…'[6] With his ironic histories, then, he only ever draws from the past something transitory that, when it is brought up, is an allegory. There are no stories or histories that the poet can narrate of what it is an allegory of; here, only the disconsolate *thought* that has neither beginnings nor ends, can help: story and history always begin and end, thoughts never, which is why we feel lifted by stories but weighed down by thoughts. And yet we pursue them. Their abysmal character hides the *secret of the world* for us, just as the wells of the past do for the poet:

> The deep well knows it certainly;
> Once all things else were deep and still,
> And all then knew their fill.⁷

The inscrutability, the groundlessness, of thought: perhaps it is closest to those who do not speak, perhaps to those who do not remember, perhaps to those who do not anticipate. But the cost of this closeness! And yet in the end, those children of the coming world who, like us, belong from the first to those who are called, are not scared off by this proximity. For them as for us, the risk of this proximity is the ungrounding danger of comprehending while losing ourselves:

> The deep well knows it certainly;
> And leaning there a man would know,
> But rising up, would lose it so,
>
> Would wildly talk, and make a song—

Deep is the well of the past, and probing this unfathomability is not for everyone. Those who do so go mad if they are fortunate; when unfortunate, they become philosophers and must endure it. Schelling was one of them; he grasped it yet sustained it and attested to the well:

> 'O past, you abyss for thought!'⁸

Today we know barely anything more about this abyss. For many, Schelling's fantastic concept of the past has itself remained in the well's depths, unattainable even for those who tried. The *secret of the world* is standardly considered well lost, and many of the more calculating even consider it better this way. Clearly, however, it is not in our gift to bring its effectiveness to a halt; even if no one knows about it any more, there is still something haunting in our heads, a nervous irritant, an inchoate longing, a conceptual febrility, that favours porous arguments and occasionally promises something, proclaiming a new epoch. One feels atavistic and readily thinks once more that the simple expression of a 'post'-feeling is enough to enable the well of the past to take its sabbath. Meanwhile: all too often, all that remains of the substance of this irritant, at first a positive phenomenon, is the driving anxiety that we are stuck in an obligatory circuit, a flight-instinct for arguments, or simply 'movement declining commitments'.[9] The contemporary presence of the world-secret has declined to the form of an irritation; its symptom: the postmodern. Nevertheless, this is a pregnant time. Perhaps not only with latecomers' births, but also with the births of those who come early. But who knows this apart from unborn children? Someone else besides? Whoever sustains knowledge:

> The deep well knows it certainly;
> Once in this lore were all men wise,
> Now but a vague dream, circling, flies.

*

Schelling, as I said, grasps this and even endures it. What he has understood by risking himself is what we will be concerned with in this book. We will of course be dealing with a thought that nowadays we require to have translated. Its terminological register has become alien to us. Therefore, we must always and repeatedly reveal what attaches to it *from the perspective of the thing itself*, in order to be able to understand what it is saying. If we keep this in view, we will take into account that Schelling requires translation, while being careful, as we must be, not to think ourselves any wiser than he if we are not to overlook completely the meditative character of certain aspects of his thinking.

Schelling is certainly a thinker whom we could in a specific sense call an analytic idealist. However, what he analytically dissects is ultimately idealism itself, and what he achieves as a by-product of this procedure is something quite different: the ideal, conceptual, rational requirements for which a meditative sensibility is a condition of access. He thus gave philosophy an entirely new means for saving the phenomena, which is precisely how Schelling, in his own way, fulfils the requirements that have always characterised the work of *great* philosophy, if we may define this as a freeing of *discourse-analytic* and *discourse-creating* energies. Each of these aspects pushes for bifurcation and autonomy. Philosophy's discourse-analytic potential acts as a court of justice for human reason, delivering its verdicts based not on a constitution issuing from a constitutional assembly, but instead focused on the unwritten constitution of successful rationality. Philosophy's discourse-creating potential acts as a culture of sensibility for *la condition humaine* that discloses, examines and makes present the deep structure of our knowledge of the world, a wealth of phenomena to which the practice of worldly engagement is blind. Both the analytic and diagnostic activity must, however, be maintained together, which is precisely what philosophy finds it most difficult to do. If we search the history of philosophy for examples of philosophers who have done justice to both aspects of philosophy, then certainly it is Aristotle we will think of first, for he was first to accomplish the impossible: to develop the analysis of discourse as discourse-creating. The name of this undertaking is *metaphysics*. Kant achieved something similar with his transcendental philosophy, as did Schelling in his *The Ages of the World*.

Yet although they are further removed from us in time, today we are still closer to Aristotle and Kant than to Schelling's bizarre speculations. How then to approach *The Ages of the World*? We can immediately discard the idea of making this work comprehensible in its own terms without following Schelling's path there, and without taking into account its development following his (failed) efforts from 1810 to 1814 to finish *The Ages of the World* as a book. Furthermore, even if we keep these framing conditions in mind, it is impossible even to grasp the intentions of the work in its own terms, insofar as these should still appear to be susceptible of systematic consideration today. This requires some generosity from us regarding Schelling's problematic. This encounter cannot reject the pattern of contemporary (analytic) philosophy, but it must expand its discourse-creative capacity in order to establish contact with Schelling's concerns. I will take the historical and systematic conditions required for a beneficial way into *The Ages of the World* into account by beginning with an introductory sketch of Schelling's thought. So that this doesn't descend into a didactic introductory lecture, I will select a particular aspect that offers a condensed presentation of Schelling's development. This aspect is Schelling's relation to Dante in the context of his efforts regarding the great didactic poem on nature (§§ 1–7).[10] I will then tackle the transition to a reconstruction of *The Ages of the World* as a construction of metaphysical problematics on the basis of the theory of predication (§§ 8–10) in order finally to enter into the reconstruction of some central ideas of *The Ages of the World* (§§ 11–20).

Finally, a few words must be said regarding how this attempt is to be understood. Naturally, I would not wish to claim that I have done justice to every facet of *The Ages of the World*. Its theological aspirations in particular have completely vanished from the systematic reconstruction. I know that some interpreters (particularly Horst Fuhrmans and Xavier Tilliette) hold precisely this to run counter to Schelling's motives and intentions, and so to be incompatible with them. For this reason, I will briefly justify the restriction. By my understanding and in accordance with its immanent method, there is no other name for Schelling's metaphysical outline of *The Ages of the World* but what could be called the *hermeneutics of predication*. That is, the explication of predicative schema as the schema of the world. Stated in such a stark *façon*, this perhaps appears somewhat grandiose, but here it simply stipulates that, considered according to its method, Schelling's metaphysics is a physics on the basis of the theory of predication. If, therefore, this methodological structure can in fact be confirmed, we then have at our disposal a key that unlocks the meaning of his metaphysics at such a level as to include all additional stocks of meaning that tower like a cathedral from this foundation, in its unexecuted ground-plan. On this basis, there is nothing arbitrary about the restriction of our reconstructive approach, but rather something fundamental.

This restriction of the concerns of our interpretation to the historical Schelling of *The Ages of the World* also defines the position of this interpretation as regards contemporary research into *The Ages of the World*. As a rule, such research has historically certainly been justified in being more ambitious. I could therefore benefit from it without having to enter into fundamental confrontation with it.[11] This is also due to the fact that such is not the ultimate purpose of this slight brush with Schelling. For reducing Schelling's metaphysical speculations to a predicative-theoretical matrix pursues the systematic interests of a recovery of metaphysical problematics for our time; an interest that undergoes only preliminary testing through this interpretation. The author is clear as to the project's weaknesses and knows that, these preliminaries notwithstanding, he is responsible for the metaphysical option, a responsibility that must face the suspicion of meaninglessness to which, after the *linguistic turn*, the metaphysics of the twentieth century is exposed.

This, however, was precisely *the* motivation for testing the metaphysical problematic in Schelling's speculations. For Schelling explored, like no other, Nietzsche included, the inner possibility of the suspicion of meaninglessness, with the result that there is absolutely no meaning that is free of this 'suspicion', if the question of what it means that something exists is posed radically enough. For the fundamental source of meaninglessness is precisely existence itself. That is to say: ultimately, what we understand by being is something prior to all meaning. For Schelling, this insight ultimately makes manifest the *world-secret* that *Being is meaningless*. The coquettishness and harshness of this formulation, which is self-erasing, is only meant to be a suggestion that the metaphysical option be removed from the front line and into the traditional conservatism regarding meaning on the part of linguistic analysis. This option, that is, claims a meaning of being that we are only able to simulate in the internal relations of linguistically manifest reasoning as inconsistency. We therefore only understand the meaning of being at the moment in which this meaning either first arises or perishes. To maintain these meaning-critical conjunctions simultaneously *in language* therefore counters meaning *in principle*. But the unavoidability of these contrary meanings is inherent in the essence of metaphysics and, in the inner circle of the meaning-conservative *milieu* of an exclusively semantic idealism,[12] can only give rise to 'suspicion'. It is not therefore a question of restoring metaphysics, but of learning to assess the metaphysical risk. For, as we can learn from Schelling, this is the same as *homo sapiens*' rationality risks.

Notes

1. Thomas Mann, *Joseph and His Brothers*, trans. John E. Woods (New York: Alfred A. Knopf, 2005), 3.
2. Thomas Mann, *The Holy Sinner*, trans. H. T. Lowe-Porter (Berkeley, CA: University of California Press, 1992), 4–5.
3. Livy, *From the Founding of the City*, trans. Benjamin Oliver Foster (Cambridge, MA: Harvard University Press, 1919).

4. Not an exact quotation. See Virgil, *Aeneid* XI 26: *Evandri primus ad urbem mittatur Pallas* ['first let Pallas be sent to Evander's mourning city'], trans. H. Rushton Fairclough (Cambridge, MA: Harvard University Press, 1959).
5. Mann, *Joseph*, 3.
6. Ibid., 3.
7. Hugo von Hofmannsthal, *The World-Secret*, in *The Lyrical Poems of Hugo von Hofmannsthal*, trans. Charles Wharton Stor (New Haven, CT: Yale University Press, 1918).
8. F. W. J. Schelling, *Die Weltalter*, ed. Manfred Schröter, 2nd edn (Munich: Beck, 1979), 218.
9. [In English in the original – tr.]
10. The text of this chapter is based on a lecture I gave on 18 October 1986 at the meeting of the German Dante Society in Krefeld. I thank the editor of the society's yearbook, Professor Marcella Roddewig, for permission to use that text (slightly altered) for this book. The entire manuscript was ultimately the foundation of a lecture on Schelling that I gave in the summer semester of 1987 at the University of Düsseldorf. My thanks to my colleague Brigitte Hamerski for her help in preparing the text for print.
11. On the literature, see Guido Schneeberger, *F.W.J. Schelling: Eine Bibliographie* (Bern: Francke, 1954); Hans-Jörg Sandkühler (ed.), *Schelling: Einführung in seine Philosophie*, 2nd edn (Stuttgart: Metzler, 1998); Hermann Zeltner, *Schelling-Forschung seit 1954* (Darmstadt: Wissenschaftliche Buchgesellschaft, 1975). On *The Ages of the World*, see Horst Fuhrmans, *Schellings Philosophie der Weltalter* (Düsseldorf: Schwann, 1954); Jürgen Habermas, *Das Absolute und die Geschichte*, dissertation, Bonn, 1954, and 'Dialectical Idealism in Transition to Materialism: Schelling's Idea of a Contraction of God and its Consequences for the Philosophy of History', trans. Nick Midgely and Judith Norman, in Judith Norman and Alistair Welchman (eds), *The New Schelling* (London: Continuum, 2004); Herman Krings, 'Das Prinzip Existenz in Schellings "*Weltaltern*"', *Symposion* 4 (1955), 335–47; Wolfgang Wieland, *Schellings Lehre von der Zeit* (Heidelberg: Winter, 1956); Josef A. Stüttler, 'Schellings Philosophie der Weltalter', *Zeitschrift für philosophische Forschung* 16 (1962), 600–15; Xavier Tilliette, *Schelling: Une philosophie en devenir*, 2nd edn, 2 vols (Paris: Vrin, 1992), ch. III: 'En marge des *Weltalter*', 541ff.; Manfred Schröter, *Kritische Studien: Über Schelling und zur Kulturphilosophie* (Munich: Oldenbourg, 1971); Lothar Zahn, *Die Sprache als Grenze der Philosophie: Eine Interpretation der Weltalter-Fragmente von F.W.J. von Schelling*, dissertation, Munich, 1957; Peter L. Oesterreich, *Philosophie, Mythos und Lebenswelt: Schellings universalihistorischer Weltalter-Idealismus und die Idee eines neuen Mythos* (Frankfurt am Main: Peter Lang, 1984), and 'Schellings Weltalter und die ausstehende Vollendung des deutschen Idealismus', *Zeitschrift für philosophische Forschung* 39 (1985), 70–85. Also indispensable are Walter Schulz, *Die Vollendung des deutschen Idealismus in der Spätphilosophie Schellings*, 2nd edn (Pfullingen: Günther Neske, 1975); Claudio Cesa, *La Filosofia Politica di Schelling* (Bari: Laterza, 1969); Manfred Frank, *Der unendliche Mangel an Sein*, 2nd edn (Munich: Fink, 1992), and *Eine Einführung in Schellings Philosophie* (Frankfurt am Main: Suhrkamp, 1985).

12. Manfred Frank is therefore entirely correct when he writes that the late Schelling's speculations are even today modern for us in the precise sense that 'a new idealism of universalised language-aptness stands dangerously close to the tradition of a semiotic correction of transcendental philosophy'. 'Editor's Introduction', Schelling, *Philosophie der Offenbarung 1841/42*, 2nd edn (Frankfurt am Main: Suhrkamp, 1993), 71.

II.

Schelling and Dante: An Introduction to Schelling's Thinking

§ 1 *Lectura dantis*

Caroline Schlegel wrote from Jena to her daughter Auguste[1] on Monday 14 October 1799: 'my dear Little Chicken … we are pushing very hard to learn Italian; every evening at 7, the devout Father Fritz [= Friedrich Schlegel, W.H.], sainted in God, gives Schelling and I a lesson. Veit is also there.'[2] Dorothea Veit, the title character of Schlegel's *Lucinde*, tells of these Italian studies as well. On 11 October 1799, she writes: 'Consummate well-being in Jena, quiet life, evenings Dante readings in the "community"'.[3] Over the course of the Dante readings, Friedrich Schlegel in turn relates to Schleiermacher on 6 January 1800 that 'I am reading Dante with him [= Schelling, W.H.] and Caroline; we have already read more than half of it, and once he has a mind for something, it is irrepressibly great.'[4]

One does not merely read Dante, one translates him, even poeticising for oneself in *terza rima* and stanzas.[5] Schelling translated the inscription over the entrance to the Inferno as well as the second canto of *Paradisio*.[6] For Christmas 1799 he wrote a great poem in stanzas, which is preserved under the title *The Heavenly Image* [*Das himmlische Bild*], a title that was later chosen for it by the editor of his oeuvre.[7] This poem directly celebrated Caroline as the second Beatrice and it is interfused with clear allusions to verses from the *Divina Commedia*.[8] This poem retains a special meaning, however, in that, according to a communication from Friedrich Schlegel to Schleiermacher,[9] it was conceived as the announcement of a great didactic poem [*Lehrgedicht*] about nature. After Herder, Goethe, above all, occupied himself with the thought of such a poem. As can be gathered from a letter from Caroline to Schelling from October 1800, Goethe, however, formally conveyed the idea for this poem directly to Schelling.[10] Decisive for such a thing was certainly the great impression that Schelling's first nature-philosophy writings had made on him, especially *The Worldsoul*, a work that appeared in 1798. Schelling had in point of fact already worked on the realisation of this nature-poem, which, at the same time, should be the epic poem of the contemporary age.[11] The meaning of this project, its claim and its philosophical legitimation, can in no way be overestimated in terms of a correct understanding of Schelling's relationship to Dante, as well as for a more profound understanding of his philosophical development after 1800. With a little tweaking, it could even be said that this nature-poem, cunningly inspired by Goethe, was, after Plato's philosophical seduction by Socrates and his departure from poesy, *the* great poetic temptation in philosophy. It took a long time for Schelling finally to resist this temptation, and the balance sheet of this resistance is, in a certain respect, his late philosophy.

Parallel to this poetic temptation, since the winter semester 1799–1800, Schelling had occupied himself in his lectures with aesthetics.[12] In Jena in the winter semester of 1802–03, he lectured on the *Philosophy of Art*.[13] The manuscript of this lecture course, which Schelling repeated in Würzburg during the winter semester of 1804–05, was edited from Schelling's posthumous writings and appeared in 1859 in the fifth volume of the first division of the *Collected Works*. In 1803 Schelling published, under the title 'On Dante in Relation to Philosophy' [*Über Dante in philosophischer Beziehung*], a self-contained treatise from this lecture course. It appeared in *Kritisches Journal der Philosophie*, which Schelling edited with Hegel (vol. 2, issue 2, 39–50, 57–62). This text does not essentially deviate from its corresponding part in the lecture course manuscript, although one finds, at the conclusion of Dante's accomplishments, a poem by Schelling in *terza rima* with the title *An Dante* [sic].[14] Independent of these writings on the philosophy of art, the *System of Transcendental Idealism*, which already appeared in 1800, developed a thoroughly spectacular theory of art in its relationship to philosophy overall.[15] For its part it refers back to Schelling's early writing, *On the Myths, Historical Dicta and Philosophemes of the Most Ancient World* (1793),[16] and, above all, to the essential thoughts of the so-called *Oldest System Programme of German Idealism* (around 1796).[17]

Although all of these writings by Schelling are of consequence for his interpretation of Dante, the Dante research restricted itself exclusively to the Dante essay and its vicinity in *The Philosophy of Art*.[18] Because of this, the assessment of Schelling's interpretation of Dante has remained understandably ambivalent. Just to name two extremes: Schelling's Dante essay was for Erich Auerbach in his 1929 essay, 'by far the most meaningful of all that was written about Dante and the *Comedy* in genuine Romanticism',[19] while Werner P. Friedrich found in 1950 that 'Schelling's appraisal of the D. C. was exalted and mystical'.[20]

Naturally a compromise formula is thinkable for these *prima vista* incompatible characterisations, because an 'exalted and mystical appraisal' can still always be 'by far the most meaningful of all that was written about Dante and the *Comedy* in genuine Romanticism'. However, such a compromise formula would only obscure the fact that the need for a compromise between these two statements is a clear indicator that a philosophical understanding of what motivated Schelling's Dante interpretation does not yet exist. It is awkward that the philosophers who expressed themselves regarding Schelling kept silent about his Dante interpretation. Indeed, what Marcella Roddeweg ascertained in 1973 still applies, namely that 'studies of Fichte's Dante interpretation,[21] and above all, Schelling's Dante interpretation, are absent on the philosophical side'. To make up for this dead loss is the task that I will work out in what follows.

Because of the complexity of this state of affairs, I will restrict myself exclusively to the question as to what meaning Dante's *Divina Commedia* has for Schelling's philosophy of art as well as for his philosophy overall.

To begin with, I will initially be concerned with grasping systematically those arguments that are the presupposition for Schelling's interest in Dante. Next, the characterisation of the interpretation of the *Divina Commedia* stimulated by these presuppositions, in order finally to address the far-reaching significance that Dante had for Schelling's philosophy overall.

§ 2 The idea of a new mythology

For the best discussion of Schelling's interpretation of Dante we remain indebted to Clara-Charlotte Fuchs's 1933 essay. It proceeds from the accurate insight that 'the most important and significant point of view on Schelling's Dante essay is his philosophical approach'.[22] For precisely this reason, and following that author, 'I turn to that work in which he engages with Dante which, of course, is the *Philosophy of Art*.'[23]

The reason for this preamble may well strike those who know Schelling as quite astonishing. For it follows from Clara-Charlotte Fuchs's entirely correct emphasis on the philosophical *façon de l'être* of Schelling's Dante interpretation that, given some knowledge of that work, we cannot engage straightaway with those texts explicitly concerned with Dante, but rather with those that first motivate his philosophical interest in Dante. Among these belong in especial degree the text written by the 17-year-old Schelling in 1792 and published in 1793, *On the Myths, Historical Dicta and Philosophemes of the Most Ancient World*. In this work Schelling proceeds from an original form of knowing in the pre-scriptural age of humanity and develops the concept of a 'mythical philosophy', that is, of the sensuous form of an original reason defined by imagination, memory and the oral tradition. This first achieves completeness in the form of a transcendental myth,[24] that is, of an explanation of nature that appeals to transcendental, supersensible forces that equally appear in person as protagonists.[25] 'Transcendental myth' therefore furnishes what would nowadays be called the animistic worldview.[26] The entire text celebrates, somewhat wildly and in ignorance of the tradition stemming from Vico, the original vitality and sensuousness of a knowing that was not yet preserved in writing, that is, literally deadened.[27]

I would very much like to understand this 1793 celebration of an original epistemic sensuousness as the burning inspiration that influences what is astonishing in the *second* of the texts pertinent in this context. I mean the demand for a new mythology as formulated in the so-called *Oldest System Programme of German Idealism* (around 1796). Although the authorship of this text remains as yet uncertain (Hegel, Schelling, or another?), its programme undoubtedly forms a missing link between Schelling's early 1793 essay *On Myths* and a *third* text by Schelling that is relevant for us before explicitly addressing Dante, namely the 1800 *System of Transcendental Idealism*. To avoid going into detail here, this process, which is completed in three steps, can be presented after the manner of a psychological stenograph:

i. The *inspiration* for the sensible form of knowing in the 1793 *Myths* is followed,
ii. in 1796, by the *programme* for a new mythology, namely a mythology of reason. This programme is finally cashed out
iii. in the *theory* of a philosophy completed mythologically by its return to the womb of poetry.

Now as a rule, programmes in philosophy suffer from arbitrary preference. It cannot therefore suffice merely to state the stages of this process. It must instead be possible to make the energy of that process palpable through an argument that is amenable to critical discussion. I reconstruct this argument on the basis of a passage from the *Oldest System Programme*,[28] and indeed as *the* argument for an aesthetic idealism with its programme of a new mythology. The argument can be recast informally into ten steps that can be divided by topic into three interconnected groups. The first articulates the romantic thesis of an original epistemic communism:

1. All knowing is originally a common good
2. The sole form in which knowing can be a common good is the aesthetic
3. The aesthetic form of knowing is mythology

From this it follows directly that all knowing is originally mythology. The next group of arguments now confronts knowing in its presently oriented state [*den Ist-Zustand des Wissens*] with elements of Kant's moral philosophy, which together may be defined as the Enlightenment thesis:

4. Knowing in modernity is merely philosophical knowing concerning reason
5. The knowing concerning reason must be realised practically
6. The practical realisation of reason is the realisation of freedom
7. The realisation of freedom presupposes that what was at first merely philosophical knowing becomes universal

Aesthetic idealism now comprises both groups, theses (1) to (7), as premises for the following inferences:

8. Modern philosophical knowing must acquire aesthetic form (follows from 7, 5 and 2)
9. The modern aesthetic form of knowing is a new mythology (follows from 8 and 3)
10. The new mythology is a mythology of reason (follows from 9 and 4)

We appreciate that the demand for a new mythology is not without rigour. As regards the status of the demand for a new mythology, minimally, three observations are to be noted:

1. The demand for a new mythology is not irrational. For the satisfaction of the demand is the presupposition of the completion of Enlightenment in the sense of its social realisation: the new mythology is Kant's practical philosophy, popularised.
2. Premise (2) is certainly characteristic of the programme of aesthetic idealism. Of course, this precise premise is not unproblematic. This is easy to see in that the thesis in itself, that is, without premises (4) to (7) that restrict it to morality, is also compatible with mythic programmes that produced such monstrous births as *The Myth of the Twentieth Century* (Rosenberg).[29] This certainly was a new mythology of which the *System Programme* would say 'the philosopher must be ashamed', since it is without doubt not a 'rational mythology' as is expressly required by (4) to (7). What the text clearly states, however, is that the decisive issue lies in explaining what the rational *is* and not in the question of the *form* of reason.
3. Against the background of considerations of premise (2), the antithesis between Schelling and Hegel becomes clear. Hegel

had originally, like Schelling (and Hölderlin), advocated premise (2). During his time at Jena (1801–07), however, he abandoned this thesis and the programme of a new mythology, in contrast to Schelling. He manifestly considered that its aestheticisation could popularise even philosophy, but only at the price of the loss of argumentation [*Deargumentisierung*]. Now if, in spite of this, a popularisation programme as mandated by the Enlightenment was maintained, then no other option would be available: a non-aesthetic form of popularisation would have to be developed. And Hegel expressly conceived of such an alternative during his Berlin period (from 1818). Picking up from the tradition of Christian Wolff's school-philosophy,[30] he outlined precisely a form of philosophy compatible with this scholastic form, that is, the encyclopaedic form. So with Schelling and Hegel, the new mythology enters into competition with the encyclopaedia as two forms for the completion of Enlightenment. Even now, it seems, this completion has not occurred.

It is equally important for our question that Schelling was convinced of the strength of this argument and that he took up the demand for a new mythology in his *System of Transcendental Idealism* (1800), in the sense that the new mythology was the medium for the return from philosophy to poesy [*Poesie*].[31] I will discuss some of the arguments for this conception below, but what is principally significant here is precisely that the mythological origin of knowledge also and unequivocally retains the function of a philosophical objective that, around 1800, is clearly consistent with Schelling's contemporaneous project for a new epic.

§ 3 The great poem about nature

Indeed, Schelling flirted with being able to bring about this new mythology in poetic form. This optimism was grounded in his view that, with his nature-philosophy already having attained the maturity of a science, it should be the precondition for its becoming poetic. The attempts at a poetic realisation of the new mythology were above all confirmed by Schelling's turn to nature-philosophy and they cannot be made comprehensible without it. The commitment to a new epic consists above all in representing the whole of the knowledge of modern times in poetic form, and the whole of this knowledge, according to Schelling's argument, would inevitably have to be knowledge of the universe. In the final analysis, in order to break through to this view, it was critical to Schelling's actual philosophical achievement at that time to blast apart Fichte's subjective idealism. Schelling realised that the cognitive achievements of the I in their transcendental scope are on the whole a facet of the character of the not-I. Expressed otherwise: it certainly counts for Kant and Fichte that we can *know* the world only insofar as we can *experience* it. But for Schelling, *that* we can do this is not in turn a property of what we can do, but rather a property of what the world can do: *world-knowledge* is in any case also a *world-event*. It is nature that brings forth the entities that can be known, and the productivity of nature is grasped through an epistemic state, and it is the achievement of the subject only in the sense that we ourselves with our knowledge are just a document of nature's self-knowing; the fact of knowing does not in any case spring forth out of the subject. According to Schelling's argument, this implies therefore that epistemology is ultimately a cosmological option inasmuch as the origination of the world has an echo in our knowledge of the world. That there is a world at all results in there being a world for us. Given that the epistemic achievement of *homo sapiens* is originally the achievement of fantasy and imagination [*Phantasie und Einbildungskraft*] and therefore has poetic origins, this primordial poesy as epistemic big bang is only the later negative big bang. As a positive big bang it has the cosmic big bang[32] as its onto-poetic prerequisite, which merely repeats itself as an event of sense [*Sinnereignis*].

Given that the energies of this onto-poetic big bang of the universe have no physical prerequisites,[33] they therefore must not be conditioned, but rather unconditioned. If it were otherwise, it would be a matter of an actual beginning of the universe. With respect to empirical astrophysics, this primordial scenario of the cosmos is only graspable speculatively, precisely as the object of speculative physics, or better: of cosmo-ontology.[34]

That unconditioned or absolute before the world, the preceding not-nature in nature, is the energy of its self-organisation: those forces that let the world be at all and also let it be temporal. At the level of the subject, these repeat themselves in every conscious achievement: they also get their energy from unconscious resources that perpetuate the self-organisation of the spirit [*Geist*]. Schelling argues that this is exactly the case in its purest form with art. Precisely for this reason is art objectively what philosophy in its conscious reconstruction can always only be subjectively: the echo of the onto-poetic energy of the world. And inasmuch, for Schelling in the 1800 *System of Transcendental Idealism*, 'art is at once the only true and eternal organon and document of philosophy'.[35] It follows from this in turn that philosophy, in the simple interest of its own objectivity, must document itself poetically.

So it was only through and through the consequence of Schelling's aesthetic idealism that he endeavoured to objectify his nature-philosophy in the form of a nature-poem. Schelling had also expressed this with beautiful clarity in his 1802–03 *Philosophy of Art*:

> The didactic poem [*Lehrgedicht*] κατ' εξοχήν can only be a poem about the universe or the nature of things. It should present the reflex of the universe in knowing. The consummate image of the universe must therefore be reached in science [...] It is certain that the science that would achive this identity with the universe, not only from the side of its matter but also from that of its form, would concur with the universe; insofar as the universe itself is the archetype [*Urbild*] of all poesy, indeed, is the poesy of the absolute itself, science in that identity with the universe would, in matter as much as in form, already in and for itself be poesy and would dissolve into poetry.[36]

§ 4 Schelling's interest in Dante

We must keep it in mind that the framework of this thought was already prepared when Schelling became acquainted with Dante through Friedrich Schlegel. What immediately fascinated him about Dante was the fact that in the *Divine Comedy*, he was dealing with a poem that, in a thought-provoking way, fulfilled all the demands of an epic of its own time that he had deduced from purely philosophical considerations as required for a new one. Schelling had set down the demands of a future form of poetry that, as he was clearly overwhelmed to note, was very nearly realised in a poem from the very beginning of the modern period. Schelling's 'irrepressible' appropriation of the *Commedia*, as Friedrich Schlegel reported to Schleiermacher,[37] doubtless stems from this astonished surprise. More specifically, it was not primarily the aesthetic qualities of the poem that enchanted Schelling, but rather its stupendous universality, based on a complete integration of the knowledge of its time. It was precisely the poetic representation of the sum total of knowledge of its time that made the *Divina Commedia* emerge for Schelling as the paradigm for a speculative epic of modern times. Homer was the beginning and is said to be the end of art, but it is Dante's *Divina Commedia* that provides the prototype for a final, Homeric form of modern knowledge. Thus, for the epic of the modern world, Schelling demands above all

> that one not lose sight of the basic characteristic of the epic: universality; that is, the transformation of everything scattered in time, and yet decisively present, into a common identity [...] One attempt of this kind began the history of modern poesy: the *Divine Comedy* of Dante.[38]

It is clear from the philosophical premises, which resulted solely from philosophical considerations on his demand for an epic of the modern period, that Schelling, in his *Philosophy of Art* and in the Dante essay of 1803, already emphasised those characteristics of the *Divina Commedia* that show its universal power. In the essay 'On Dante in Relation to Philosophy', Schelling once again formulated what was for him the guiding point of view: 'The energy with which a particular individual shapes the particular combination of the available materials of his life and times determines the extent to which it receives mythological force.'[39] Dante's poem is assessed on this basis, with the result that:

> In this respect Dante is archetypal, since he has expressed what the modern poet must do in order to set down in its entirety and in a poetic whole the history and culture of his time and the particular mythological material that is before him. He must combine the allegorical and the historical with absolute freedom of choice [*Willkür*].[40]

Only this freedom of choice guarantees that the poem fuses with the author, that the author becomes universal through his poetry, the individual identical with his world. This perspective also steers Schelling's statements on the question of genre. Here too the *Commedia* attests to its universality and uniqueness, since it cannot 'be subsumed under any other genre'. The poem

> is not an epic, it is not a didactic poem, it is not a novel in the real sense, it is not even a comedy or drama such as Dante himself called it. It is the most indissoluble mixture, the most complete interpenetration of everything [...] rather, as a genre it is itself the most universal representative of modern poesy, not an individual poem, but the poem of all poems, the poesy of modern poesy itself.[41]

Schelling's celebration of Dante is clear and palpable. But while celebrating Dante, he is simultaneously praising the *Divina Commedia* as the unforeseen verification of his theory of a new mythology. Or more precisely: he prizes it as evidentiary for the historical possibility of the new mythology. On this view, the *Divina Commedia* retains something simultaneously archetypal and preliminary. It stands for what is to come; it is itself not yet 'there', where it refers to. At the same time, however, it does not only refer, but rather its form prefigures what is to come. If Schelling became increasingly assured that, with his account of Dante's poem he 'had shown that it is prophetic, archetypal, for all modern poesy',[42] fundamentally he offered a typological interpretation of the *Divina Commedia*: he understood it as the type of a poetry of the future that will only become the fulfilment of that poetry's prophetic promise as its antitype.

Over and above these findings, and so as not merely to repeat here Clara-Charlotte Fuchs's authoritative and detailed commentary, there would now be nothing more to say concerning Schelling's essay 'On Dante in Relation to Philosophy', precisely in relation to philosophy, if things did not – unfortunately – lie far deeper than has been anticipated up to now.

§ 5 Schelling's task of a poetic version of the new mythology

In his last year in Jena (1802–03), Schelling was almost stunned by the idea that the preparatory work for the new mythology had already been provided by his nature-philosophy. In any case, he does not leave the slightest doubt about this self-estimation: 'Neither do I hide my conviction that in nature-philosophy [...] the first, distant foundation has been laid for that future symbolism and mythology that will be created not by an individual but rather by the entire age.'[43] Indeed, Schelling in his philosophical writings never claimed *more* than precisely this: to have created with his nature-philosophy a *condition* for the new mythology. This also holds for the time in which he secretly undertook thoroughgoing poetic attempts towards its realisation. In a poem (*Lebenskunst* or *The Art of Life*) from 1802, in contrast, Schelling speaks, in accord with an ancient prototype, as a divinely inspired evangelist [*Lehrverkünder*], who is far more elevated than he is as a philosopher:

> Die goldnen Lehren hört aus treuem Munde,
> Wie sie ein Gott mir selbst hat eingegeben,
> Empfangt von mir des Lebens sichre Kunde.
>
> Hearing the golden teachings from faithful mouths,
> As though a god has given them to me Himself,
> The sure tidings of life received by me.[44]

Schelling had abandoned his efforts to write the great didactic poem by 1809 (the death of Caroline) at the very latest. The 1807 lecture *On the Relationship of the Plastic Arts to Nature* already explicitly announced the insight into the impossibility of a fusion of philosophy and poetry. 'Art and Science', it says here decidedly, 'can both only revolve around their own axes.'[45] Philosophy appears here merely as an indicator of a prospective art that therefore now alone takes over the function of a cultural final gestalt. In this speech, given on the occasion of the name day of the king on 12 October 1807, Schelling gives this reduced hope a national colouring indebted to the occasion: 'This people, which emerged from the revolution in the mindset of a new Europe [...] this people must culminate in an art peculiar to them.'[46]

I first found explicit evidence for the definitive task of the project of a new mythology *as* the fusion of philosophy and poesy in Schelling's *Erlangen Lectures* from the winter semester of 1820–21: 'Why is philosophy not, in accord with both the word and its meaning, merely history (ἱστορία), or narration? – That would be the long intimated golden age, where fable also becomes truth.'

And now it means, immediately and with great severity, to scramble to get, so to speak, jerkily out of the seductive dream and into this dream that long ago stopped being dreamed. 'Yet this is impossible.'[47] Impossible therefore, according to Schelling's late argument, because a philosophy merged with narration remains only narration: 'it would only bring us to a dead historical knowing'.[48] For a philosophy merged with poetry separates philosophy from what it de facto exclusively receives from life; philosophy separates itself from interpretative acts and cedes its arguments to externally posited images that may well have meaning but that can no longer be critically tested.

This fact only implies that Schelling gave up the idea of a poetic realisation of the new mythology sometime between the years 1804 and 1809; it does not imply at the same time that he had relinquished the idea of a new mythology. Rather it is the case that, in lieu of the abandoned poetic project, there is now a prosaic one, namely, the veritably gigantic project, *The Ages of the World*, which Schelling conceived in continuously renewed drafts from 1810 until 1814, and which he pursued even further. He also failed at the prosaic solution to a new mythology, but not because he lacked the prosaic energies as he had earlier lacked the poetic energies – these were always at his disposal in a virtuoso manner – but rather because of objective [*sachlich*] reasons; in any case, it is honourable that he had penetrated so deeply overall that he could fail for such reasons. Of the three planned books of *The Ages of the World*, namely, *The Past*, *The Present* and *The Future*, Schelling had only worked through the first book, the various versions of which were only available in galleys; without exception nothing of it was published by Schelling.

The Ages of the World, however, offers its own testimony that it still belongs to Schelling's efforts towards a prosaic new mythology. Schelling once again, quailing with melancholy, says as much in the introduction, and immediately yields this vision to the future author of a consummate form of the new mythology. The *Oldest System Programme* intimated that this future author would be the *founder of a religion*; the *System of Transcendental Idealism* intimated that the author would be a *poet* who represents a generation. Finally, *The Ages of the World*, sublating both, ultimately models itself on an ancient oracle:

> Perhaps the one is still coming who will sing the greatest heroic poem, grasping in spirit something for which the seers of old were famous: what was, what is, what will be. But this time has not yet come. We must not misjudge our time. Heralds of this time, we do not want to pick this fruit before it is ripe nor do we want to misjudge what is ours [...] We cannot be narrators, only explorers...[49]

At any rate, whenever *The Ages of the World* is presented as a proclamation of a new age, it is explicitly meant as the preliminary form of the new mythology, which is presented speculatively as something merely temporary and still absent, but in which there is still green fruit.

The question that therefore must still occupy us here is: Is Dante's archetypal role for the new mythology, which Schelling so emphatically celebrated in 1803, blinded by the task of its poetic composition, or is it still compatible with the prosaic and temporary version of the new mythology in the form of *The Ages of the World*? Indeed, this question is difficult to answer because the name Dante is not found in *The Ages of the World*, so that one has to embark on an analysis of what this strange trunk contains, which is nothing short of foolhardy. For what Schelling himself in the *Erlangen Lectures* quoted as a warning, citing Dante (in his own translation) one last time, is also valid here: 'What Dante let be written on the gate to the Inferno can also in another sense be written on the entrance to philosophy: Abandon hope, all you who enter here.'[50]

§ 6 Dante as archetype for *The Ages of the World*

In his Dante essay, Schelling had already indicated that 'the trichotomy in Dante for a higher, prophetic poesy, which expressed an entire era' is 'thinkable as a universal form'.[51] He had already emphasised that the 'division of the universe and the arrangement of material in accordance with the three domains – *infernum, purgatorium*, and paradise' exhibits a 'universal symbolic form' entirely independent of Christianity.[52] Now briefly stated, my thesis is first of all that the trichotomy of the *Divina Commedia*, even in the qualities of these three domains, remained structurally archetypal for the three parts conceived for *The Ages of the World*:

The Past corresponds to *Inferno*, *The Present* to *Purgatorio* and *The Future* to *Paradiso*.[53] In a certain regard we could therefore call *The Ages of the World* the divine comedy of time, or, as Schelling himself calls it, a 'genealogy of time'[54] or the 'great system of times'.[55] Of course, it is clear that nothing much is gained by the assertion that Dante's trichotomy is archetypal for *The Ages of the World* unless it is shown that there are indications of Dante's influence on the content.

We must first draw attention to a characteristic of *The Ages of the World*, of which Dante's *Divina Commedia* is certainly not the cause, but which is common to both works: this does not of course supply their *raison d'être*, but they are, by way of their *façon de parler*, popular interventions in the most exacting sense. Once Schelling had abandoned the aesthetic constitution of his philosophy in the form of a poem, he explicitly chose a 'popular' prose to meet the *System Programme*'s old demand for a form of philosophy also understood by the people. Dante's reasoning for composing his great poem in the mother tongue here has a counterpart in Schelling's reasoning:

> The language of the system is yesterday's, that of the people as though from eternity. I therefore think that the time has come when whoever has engaged with the highest science owes the fruit of their researches more to the world and its peoples than to the school.[56]

Now, since Schelling's argument directly opposes the language of the people to the artificial language of his nature-philosophy, the new work cannot fail to have its desired effect, for 'popularity, which is so often sought in vain, will then come on its own'.[57] *The Ages of the World* is therefore explicitly conceived as *pop* philosophy, although the reader may be astonished to hear this. For upon entering the inferno of the past with its God-starved ontogenesis and chronogenesis, this birthing chamber of being, this sputtering ontology of the will, one is immediately subject to a bewildering vertigo. In fact, whoever ventures into *The Ages of the World* and is easily pulled down by it does not possess what Schelling quite rightly demands from the outset: a strong soul.[58] And so, in the sketches for the first book of *The Ages of the World*, at the beginning of that infernal speculation on the abyss of the past, there is a clear reminder of the regard for Dante when Schelling says that here we are 'embarking on the long, dark path of the ages from the very beginning'.[59] Here 'from the very beginning' means still behind a first being, which in consequence comes to be from a dimension prior to time, that is, from eternity. Yet this process can only start as all processes can only start: there must be an energetic difference. Since physical energies cannot yet be taken into consideration here, it can only be dealing with a difference of logical energy, that is, with a contradiction.

Schelling takes this contradiction as the eternal Yes and No, which initially without affirming force are indifferent to one another. Yes and No first charge a contradiction when they repel one another. Schelling takes this antagonism as the contradiction in God and asks: 'How is one to reconcile this contradiction?'[60] Now since it is evident that 'God as the Yes and God as the No cannot have being *at the same time*',[61] identity permeates eternity, and the times arise with which God's consistency with himself remains guaranteed. Primal contradiction generates time.

> Hence, the contradiction only breaks with eternity when it is in its highest intensity and, instead of a single eternity, posits a succession of eternities (eons) or times. But this succession of eternities is precisely what we, by and large, call time.[62]

Schelling also conceives of God's antagonistic past, which is ultimately generative of time and being,[63] as the 'orgasm of forces',[64] as the 'inner self-laceration of nature, that wheel of initial birth spinning about itself as if mad',[65] and as 'the self-lacerating madness [that] is still now what is innermost in all things […] the real force of nature and of all its products'.[66] Schelling especially presents this fundamental madness through the image of the turning wheel, and we know that Schelling was here inspired by Jacob Böhme.[67] The question, however, is whether it was *only* Böhme from whom he inherited this metaphor. For Schelling, just like Böhme, first took the measure of 'the wheel of the planets' with this image.[68] Further, only the eternal Yes applies a brake to the fast-turning wheel of the eternal No, and only thus is it productive of being and time. And Schelling conceives this eternal Yes as the love that onto-creatively assuages the eternal No as God's fury: 'Nature is nothing other than divine egoism, softly and gently subdued by love.'[69] If we assess all this evidence together, Schelling's divine wheel[70] also appears to refer to the last lines of the *Divina Commedia*:

> ma già volgeva il mio disio e 'l velle,
> si come ruota ch'igualmente è mossa,
> l'amor che move il sole e l'altre stelle.[71]

This kinship becomes even clearer when the world-forming energy dispersed throughout the structures of time [*Zeitgestalten*] finally, in the outline of the third book, are integrated into one great 'simultaneity between whatever has come into being, so that the fruits of various times live reunited in one time, circling about like leaves and organs of one and the same flower, all gathered together around one point in the middle'.[72]

Already in 1954, Manfred Schröter wrote of this temporally final state of being that it 'cannot help but [recall] another, powerful, poetic symbol: Dante's Rose of Heaven'.[73] That this comparison between Schelling's 'flower' and Dante's Rose of Heaven is not merely an isolated association is due above all to the fact that Dante, in the all-consuming glimpse into the depths of the Rose of Heaven, creates an inexpressible experience of presence. For in its depths –

> Legato con amore in un volume,
> Ciò che per l'universo si squaderna –[74]

everything is simultaneously present. And Schelling conceives precisely this presence as 'the simultaneity of all becomings'. Thus, Dante's Rose of Heaven and Schelling's Flower of Time are sculptures of one great 'at once [*Zumal*]', in which everything is gathered: the ultimate congress of being and time. In this vision once again there resonates what Schelling, in the *Philosophy of Art*, designated as the presupposition of the new epic, which is, that is, only possible when 'the one thing after another of the modern world has transformed itself into a *simultaneity*'.[75] He then interpreted Dante's poem as evidence that this presupposition can be met. That Dante's spirit also leaves structurally formative traces in Schelling's *The Ages of the World* attests to the fact that Dante's significance for Schelling in relation to philosophy is only understood in its depths. Of course, we have not yet thereby gained anything as regards the philosophical or argumentational legitimacy of *The Ages of the World*. For as Schelling writes in the Introduction to *The Ages of the World*, 'not only poets, but also philosophers, have their ecstasies'.[76] Indeed, 'there is no understanding in vision in and for itself'.[77] That is, without reconstructing its argument, *The Ages of the World* remains what it has long since been: an imposing document of the history of spirit, but only that.

§ 7 The task of an argumentative reconstruction of *The Ages of the World*

But since there can be no doubt that the philosophical meaning of *The Ages of the World*, as well as Schelling's late philosophy overall, stands or falls with its capacity to be reconstructed, I would like to provide a clue to the supposed key for this task. It is a key that Schelling himself handed over, without anyone, so far as I can see, having picked up on it.[78]

First of all, without any ifs or buts, *access* to Schelling's mature metaphysics can only be found in the starting point of a theory of predication. Schelling himself repeatedly moved such a theory of judgement into the foreground. *The Ages of the World* explicitly states that 'the knowledge of the general laws of judgment ... [must] always accompany the supreme science'.[79] In the draft of the first book of the 1813 version, Schelling also wrote that 'although knowledge of the universal laws of judging by no means constitutes the highest science itself, it is so essentially interconnected with the highest science that they cannot be separated'.[80]

Secondly, Kant's doctrine of the transcendental ideal (*CPR* B 599ff.) is reconstructed in this theory of predication since this doctrine is already the *clavis*[81] to an understanding of Schelling's metaphysics. He himself had seen it this way until the end and still explicitly spoke of it in his lecture to the Berlin Academy of Sciences on 17 January 1850! In this lecture, Schelling grasped God as an *ens realissimum* in Kant's sense, that is, to use the language of modern philosophy, as an absolute proposition: 'Kant therefore shows that the idea of the overall *possibility* or sum total [*Inbegriff*] of all predicates belongs to the intellectual determination of things [= every identification in terms of predication, W.H.]'.[82] Schelling explicitly refers in this lecture to the lectures from his *Philosophy of Mythology* 'that I likewise had the honor of delivering here'.[83] More precisely, this is the lecture, 'On Kant's Ideal of Pure Reason', which he delivered to the Berlin Academy on 15 March and 29 April 1847 (= the eleventh and the twelfth lecture of the *Philosophy of Mythology*). A note from the text of the twelfth lecture reads:

> But there are numerous historiographers, who for some time found the latest philosophy nothing less than being aware of the just mentioned genetic connection [with Kant's philosophy, W.H.] and, not having reckoned with it, imagine that everything later is just something accidental, arbitrary, and ungrounded that goes beyond Kant. They are finally less discerning and at least not in the position to specify the point in the house of Kantian criticism in which the later development concludes as a necessary consequence. This point in my opinion can be found in Kant's doctrine of the ideal of reason.[84]

In my opinion, only with this key can Schelling's late philosophy finally liberate itself from its reputation as the 'theosophical buffoonery of the philosophical Cagliostro of the Nineteenth Century' (Feuerbach).[85] I say: it *can* succeed, but there is no guarantee that it will. For it could also be that he is still too far ahead of us. For who has posed the 'necessary question' with the radicality of the late Schelling: 'Why sense at all, why not nonsense instead of sense?'[86] And how far beyond modernity is he when he ascertains: 'The whole world is, so to speak, caught in reason, but the question is: how did it get in this net …?'[87]

Notes

1. Caroline's daughter from her first marriage to the doctor J. F. W. Böhmer.
2. *Caroline: Briefe aus der Frühromantik*, ed. Erich Schmidt, vol. 1, reprint edn (Bern: Herbert Lang, 1970), 565–6. [The first edition appeared in two volumes in Leipzig with Insel Verlag in 1913 – tr.]
3. Communicated by Erich Schmidt in *Caroline: Briefe aus der Frühromantik*, 743 n.247.
4. *Aus Schleiermachers Leben*, ed. Ludwig Jonas and Wilhelm Dilthey, 4 vols (Berlin: Georg Reimer, 1860–63). The citation is from vol. 3, 146. See also *Aus Schellings Leben: In Briefen*, ed. Gustav Leopold Plitt (Leipzig: S. Hirzel, 1869), 289n.

5. It emerges from her letter of 6 January 1800 that Dorothea Veit, Friedrich Schlegel and Schelling had developed a taste for this form of verse: 'And what will you first say when you hear that I, I *myself*, have brought these furious and fervent stanzas upon our house.' *Caroline und Dorothea Schlegel in Briefen*, ed. Ernst Wieneke (Weimar: Gustav Kiepenheuer Verlag, 1914).
6. [SW I/10, 441–6.]
7. [See SW I/10, 531 and n.]
8. Concerning this, see the supporting documents in Hans Kunz, *Schellings Gedichte und dichterische Pläne*, dissertation (Zürich: Juris-Verlag, 1955), 61–2.
9. Plitt (ed.), *Aus Schellings Leben*, 289n.
10. Schmidt (ed.), *Caroline: Briefe aus der Frühromantik*, vol. 2, 6: 'Goethe also now conveys the poem to you; he hands his nature down to you. Since he cannot make you his heir, he makes a donation to you among the living.'
11. Whether this project of a didactic poem about nature always coincides with the vision of a contemporary epic still needs to be examined.
12. Concerning this, see *F. W. J. Schelling: Briefe und Dokumente*, ed. Horst Fuhrmans, vol. 1 (Bonn: H. Bouvier, 1962), 174 n.24, 235. Volume 2 appeared in 1973 and volume 3 in 1975.
13. For the background of this lecture announcement, see Plitt (ed.), *Aus Schellings Leben*, 375. Concerning this, see Fuhrmans (ed.), *Briefe und Dokumente*, vol. 2, 412 n.11. Incidentally, on 3 September 1802 Schelling invited August Wilhelm Schlegel for the preparation of this lecture course. Schelling had seen his lecture manuscript, *On Fine Literature and Art* [*Über schöne Literatur und Kunst*], while on a visit to Berlin in May 1802, but he had not studied it carefully [Fuhrmans (ed.), *Briefe und Dokumente*, vol. 2, 435, 436 n.15 – tr.].
14. Cf. *Schellings sämmtliche Werke* (Stuttgart/Augsburg: Cotta, 1861), division 1, vol. 10, 441. [Hogrebe cites Manfred Schröter's 1927 re-edition of Schelling's works according to the revised order of its particular volumes, which Schröter divided between 'Hauptbände' and 'Ergänzungsbände', rather than according to the SW pagination that Schröter's edition reproduces. For the reader's ease of reference, we have given the standard pagination according to K. F. A. Schelling (ed.), *Schellings Werke* (Stuttgart and Augsburg, 1856–61, 14 vols). This citation thus reads SW I/10, 441. An English translation of the Dante essay can be found in 'On Dante in Relation to Philosophy', hereafter 'On Dante', trans. Elizabeth Rubenstein and David Simpson, in *The Origins of Modern Critical Thought: German Aesthetics and Literary Criticism from Lessing to Hegel*, ed. David Simpson (Cambridge: Cambridge University Press, 1988), 239–47. For the original lecture version of the essay, see Schelling, *The Philosophy of Art*, ed. and trans. Douglas W. Stott (Minneapolis, MN: University of Minnesota Press, 1989), 239–47 – tr.]
15. Concerning this, cf. the beautiful study by Dieter Jähnig, *Schelling: Die Kunst in der Philosophie*, 2 vols (Pfullingen: Neske, 1966 and 1969).
16. [SW I/1, 41–84. Hereafter 'Myths'.]
17. The text is cited from the copy in Fuhrmans (ed.), *Briefe und Dokumente*, vol. 1, 69–71.
18. Cf. among others, Erich Auerbach, *Entdeckung Dantes in der Romantik*, in *Deutsche Vierteljahrsschrift für Literaturwissenschaft und Geistesgeschichte* VII, 4

(1929), 682–92; Clara-Charlotte Fuchs, 'Dante in der deutschen Romantik', *Deutsches Dante-Jahrbuch* 15 (Weimar: Verlag Böhlau, 1933), 61–131; Werner P. Friedrich, *Dante's Fame Abroad* (Rome: Edizioni di Storia e Letteratura, 1950), esp. 461–5.
19. Auerbach, *Entdeckung Dantes in der Romantik*, 690.
20. Ibid., 462.
21. [Fichte translated some parts of the *Divina Commedia*. See J. G. Fichte, 'Dantes irdisches Paradies (Übersetzung)', in *Gesamtausgabe der Bayerischen Akademie der Wissenschaften*, vol. 9, *Werke 1806–1807*, ed. Reinhard Lauth and Hans Gliwitzky (Stuttgart: Frommann-Holzboog, 1993), 279ff. See also Hugo Daffner, 'Fichte als Dante Übersetzer', *Deutsches Dante-Jahrbuch* 9 (Weimar: Verlag Böhlau 1925).]
22. Fuchs, 'Dante in der deutschen Romantik', 90.
23. Ibid. [The author is referring to Schelling's 1802 lectures on *The Philosophy of Art* – tr.]
24. [SW I/1, 76–8.] The term 'transcendental' should be read as 'transcendent', and not therefore in Kant's sense.
25. [SW I/1, 77.] 'Transcendental myth in general is the exhibition of a transcendental object through a fact invented poetically [*gedichtetes*] in time.'
26. Schelling attempts a psychological explanation of the genesis of the animistic worldview: 'Of course, had humanity ever suspected that there remained something on the far side of appearances that the eye had not seen nor the ear heard […] small wonder that he vitalized the entirety of nature around him, small wonder that, in each of the manifold forms in which nature revealed itself to him, the richer and more manifold the mythology he propagated' [SW I/1, 77].
27. Naturally, Paul is in the background here (2 Corinthians 3:6). Schelling also extends this to legal texts: 'Should one of the tribe sin, one does not refer him to a cold, dead law, but rather to a living example from former ages…' [SW I/1, 80].
28. 'Before we make the ideas aesthetic, i.e., mythological, they are of no interest to the *people* and on the other hand, before mythology is rational, the philosopher must be ashamed of it. Thus enlightened and unenlightened must shake hands, mythology must become philosophical and the people rational, and philosophy must become mythological in order to make the philosophers sensuous. Then eternal unity will reign among us. Never the despising gaze, never the blind trembling of the people before its wise men and priests. Only then can we expect the *same* development of *all* forces, of the individual as well as all individuals. No force will be suppressed any more, then general freedom and equality of spirits shall reign!' In Fuhrmans (ed.), *Briefe und Dokumente*, vol. 1, 71. [Trans. Andrew Bowie in *Aesthetics and Subjectivity* (Manchester: Manchester University Press, 1990), 266–7 – tr.]
29. [Alfred Rosenberg was a Nazi ideologue. His *Der Mythus des zwanzigsten Jahrhunderts* (Munich: Hoheneichen, 1930) argued for a hierarchy of races, with the Caucasoid Aryans at its head. The titular 'myth' the book proposed was to be a 'blood-awakening' to this hierarchy.]
30. Joachim Ritter has clearly brought out Hegel's recourse to the philosophy of the schools. See his *Metaphysik und Politik* [*Metaphysics and Politics*] (Frankfurt am Main: Suhrkamp, 1969), 259 n.3, 281 n.1.

31. According to Schelling, then, the conclusion to be drawn is that 'philosophy was born and nourished by poesy [*Poesie*] in the infancy of science [*Wissenschaft*], and with it all those sciences it has guided toward completion; we may thus expect them, on completion, to flow back like so many individual streams into the universal ocean of poesy from which they took their source. Nor is it in general difficult to say what the medium for this return to poesy will be; for in mythology such a medium existed [...]' [SW I/3, 629; trans. Peter Heath, *System of Transcendental Idealism* (Charlottesville, VA: University Press of Virginia, 1978), hereafter *System*, 232, translation slightly modified – tr.].
32. 'We assume then, that the universe brought itself forth [...] by means of an always advancing explosion' (*Erster Entwurf eines Systems der Naturphilosophie* (1799) [SW I/3, 120; trans. Keith R. Peterson, *First Outline of a System of the Philosophy of Nature* (Albany, NY: State University of New York Press, 2004), hereafter *First Outline*, 89 – tr.].
33. 'I urge the reader not to think of mechanical forces when I use this expression [an always advancing explosion, W.H.], which began to operate much later in Nature' [SW I/3, 122 n.1; *First Outline*, 90].
34. 'As science cannot set out from anything that is a product, that is, a thing, it must set out from the unconditioned [...] Inasmuch as everything of which we can say that it *is*, is of a conditioned nature, it is only *being itself* that can be unconditioned' [*Erster Entwurf*, SW I/3, 283; *First Outline*, 201–2].
35. [SW I/2, 627; *System*, 231, translation slightly modified.]
36. Schelling continues: 'The origin of the absolute didactic poem or of the speculative epic therefore coincides with the consummation of science, and just as science first came from poetry, it is also its most beautiful and ultimate determination, to flow back into this ocean' [SW I/5, 666–7, our translation; see also *The Philosophy of Art*, 226].
37. Plitt (ed.), *Aus Schellings Leben*, 289n.
38. [SW I/5, 685–6; *The Philosophy of Art*, 238–9.]
39. [SW I/5, 156; 'On Dante', 242.]
40. [SW I/5, 156; 'On Dante', 242.]
41. [SW I/5, 686–7; *The Philosophy of Art*, 239.]
42. [SW I/5, 163; 'On Dante', 247, translation slightly modified.]
43. [SW I/5, 449; *The Philosophy of Art*, 76, translation slightly modified.]
44. [I/10, 439.] This poem otherwise stands in the tradition of Schelling's earlier poem, *Epikurisch Glaubensbekenntniß Heinz Widerporstens* (cf. Plitt (ed.), *Aus Schellings Leben*, vol. 1, 282–9).
45. [SW I/7, 327; trans. Michael Bullock, in Herbert Read, *The True Voice of Feeling* (London: Faber, 1953), hereafter *Arts and Nature*, 355.]
46. [SW I/7, 328; *Arts and Nature*, 357, translation slightly modified.] Regarding this address, cf. Lucia Sziborsky, 'Schelling und die Münchener Akademie der bildenden Künste', *Hegel-Studien*, supplement 27 (1986), 39–64.
47. Schelling, *Initia Philosophæ Universæ: Erlanger Vorlesung WA 1820/21*, ed. Horst Fuhrmans (Bonn: Bouvier, 1969), 49.
48. Ibid.
49. [SW I/8, 206; trans. Jason M. Wirth, *The Ages of the World* (Albany, NY: State University of New York Press, 2000), hereafter *Ages*, xl.]
50. Schelling, *Initia Philosophæ Universæ*, 19. Schelling here anticipates Husserl's *epoché* because the text further reads: 'Who truly wants to philosophize must give up all hope, all desire, all yearning [*Sehnsucht*]; he must want nothing,

know nothing, and feel altogether bare and poor, leaving everything behind in order to gain everything.'
51. [SW I/5: 158; 'On Dante', 243.]
52. [SW I/5: 157; 'On Dante', 243.]
53. Marcella Roddeweg pointed out to me that, in its compact form, this thesis could be misunderstood, as it makes it appear that the three parts of the *Divina Commedia* are equated with the vulgar understanding of temporal process (past, present, future), which naturally runs counter to Dante's statements. In point of fact, the relation is that the *Inferno* corresponds to *The Ages of the World*'s past in the sense that the past which Schelling addresses is pre-time, the eternal past, from which times are delivered, without positing an end for it. Pre-time remains constantly present as something merely 'repressed'. To this extent, Schelling's past claims of itself exactly what is written above Dante's *Inferno* (III, 6–8):

> *facemi la divina potestate,*
> *la somma spienza e il primo amore.*
> *Dinanzi a me non fur cosa create*
> *se non eterne, ed io eterno duro* ...

> [I am a creature of the Holiest Power, / of Wisdom in the Highest and of Primal Love. / Nothing till I was made was made, only / eternal beings. And I endure eternally.]

Manfred Schröter was the first to refer to this connection: 'Thus, in these remarkable opening pages, as it were, through the monumental portal of his work, upon which were previously chiselled, albeit in another sense, Dante's immortal words: *Facemi* [...] recalling the words that Schelling, in one of his most comprehensive revisions and, breathing again while looking back over the whole, wrote after the last line:

> *O past, you abyss of thoughts!*

(*Schellings sämmtliche Werke, Nachlaßband* [hereafter, *Weltalter*], Editor's Introduction, xviii). Nevertheless, I would like to emphasise that the comparison of *The Ages of the World* and the *Divina Commedia* can in general claim the status of just one perspective that does no more than make a structural impulse apparent, albeit one characteristic of the claims of *The Ages of the World*. Finally, as an alternative to Dante, one could make Joachim of Fiore [a twelfth-century abbot whose millennial theory of history divided it into 'three ages' (of the Father, the Son, and the Holy Spirit) – tr.] a valid archetype for Schelling's trichotomy in *The Ages of the World*; but this is simply ruled out, because at the time of composing *The Ages of the World* fragments, Schelling knew nothing about Joachim's existence, and was first introduced to him by Johann August Wilhelm Neander's *Allgemeine Geschichte der christlichen Religion und Kirche* [*Universal History of the Christian Religion and the Church*, 6 vols (Hamburg: Perthes, 1825ff.)], as he himself explains in the 36th lecture of his *Philosophy of Revelation*. See here Karl Löwith, *Weltgeschichte und Heilsgeschehen* (Stuttgart: Metzler, 1979), 192–3, Appendix 1: *Transformations in Joachim's Doctrine*.
54. *Weltalter* (Draft I) [trans. Joseph P. Lawrence, *The Ages of the World* (*1811*) (Albany, NY: State University of New York Press, 2019), hereafter *Ages 1811*, 135], 75.

55. *Weltalter* (Draft I), 14 [*Ages 1811*, 70].
56. *Weltalter* (fragment for Book 1), 224.
57. *Weltalter* (Draft II), 118 [trans. Judith Norman, in Slavoj Žižek, *The Abyss of Freedom*/F. W. J. Schelling, *The Ages of the World* (Ann Arbor, MI: University of Michigan Press, 1997), hereafter *Ages 1813*, 119]. At this point the programme of a new mythology, with its utopian impetus, comes once again to the fore: 'There will then no longer be a difference between the world of thought and the world of actuality [*Wirklichkeit*]. The world will be one, with the peace of the golden age heralded in the harmonious connection of all the sciences.'
58. [SW I/8, 207; *Ages*, 3.]
59. *Weltalter* (Draft I), 14 [*Ages 1811*, 70, translation slightly modified to include the phrase '*von Anbeginn*' on which Hogrebe here comments – tr.].
60. [SW I/8, 301; *Ages*, 75.]
61. [SW I/8, 302; *Ages*, 76.]
62. [SW I/8, 302; *Ages*, 76.]
63. *The Ages of the World* is, as a whole, a treatise on the 'reasoning of the ever-existing God, concerning the god which was one day to be existent (τόν πότε ἐσόμενον θεόν)'. Plato, *Timaeus* 34a-b [trans. R. G. Bury (Cambridge, MA: Harvard University Press, 1929)].
64. [SW I/8, 336; *Ages*, 100.]
65. [SW I/8, 337; *Ages*, 103.]
66. [SW I/8, 338; *Ages*, 103.]
67. Cf. in particular Horst Fuhrmans, *Schelling's Philosopie der Weltalter* [*Schelling's Philosophy of the Ages of the World*] (Düsseldorf: Schwann, 1954). [For Böhme's 'wheel of the planets', see e.g. *The Signature of All Things*, ed. Clifford Bax (London: Dent, 1912), iv, 33: 'And as the eternal birth is in itself in the heavenly Mercury, *viz*. in the eternal word in the Father's generation; so likewise with the motion of the Father it came into a creaturely being, and so proceeds in its order, as may be seen in the wheel of the planets' – tr.]
68. *Weltalter* (Draft I), 38 [*Ages 1811*, 97].
69. *Weltalter* (Draft I), 85 [*Ages 1811*, 145]. The strict connection between the wheel and love is also attested to by a poem of Schelling's from the year 1812 (24 December), under the title *To the Beloved*, that is, to Pauline Gotter. The poem makes reference to Schelling's seal, which represents a sphinx holding a wheel under its right paw. (See K. F. A. Schelling's Editor's note to SW I/10, 451. A reproduction is given above, p. 00. I thank Dr Walter Schieche of the Bavarian Academy of the Sciences for the photograph.) The poem runs:

> Doch erblickst du das Rad, das unter der Tatze sich wendet,
> Deut' es mir schalkeitsvoll nicht auf Veränderlichkeit,
> Deut' es auf innerer Liebe Beständigkeit, selige Ruhe,
> In der Bewegung der Welt, unter dem Wechsel der Zeit.
> [Now you see the wheel turning beneath the paw,
> To me it does not slyly point to mutability,
> It points to the constancy of inner love, blissful rest,
> In the movement of the world, beneath changing time.]

70. Dante's lines are ultimately of Aristotelian inspiration and this, according to its materials, sets limits to a comparison with Schelling's figuration. But nor will I here set these thoughts entirely to one side. At any rate, it was

not at all only from Jacob Böhme that Schelling inherited this image; his language expressly echoes James 3:6 (ὁ τροχὸν τῆς γενέσεως [the wheel of generation]), Heraclitus (ἀκάματον πῦρ [unresting fire]) and then clearly formulates it in the Stoic tradition. [See SW I/8, 231; *Ages* 21.]
71. 'But my desire and will, like wheels of carts / That evenly are rolled, was moved by might / Of love, which sways the sun and all the stars'. *Paradise* XXXIII, 143–5.
72. *Weltalter* (Draft I), 87 [*Ages 1811*, 148].
73. Manfred Schröter, 'Mythopoese' [*Mythopoiesis*], *Studia Philosophica* 14 (1954): 202–10, here 208 n.18.
74. *Paradiso* xxxiii, 86–7. Schröter refers correctly to this verse. [By love bound up together in one whole, / All that which through the universe doth churn.]
75. [SW I/5:445; *The Philosophy of Art*, 75, translation slightly modified.]
76. [SW I/8, 203; *Ages*, xxxviii.]
77. [SW I/8, 203; *Ages*, xxxviii.]
78. A clear exception, because it was pursuing a different objective, is the work of Erhard Oeser, *Die Antike Dialektik in der Spätphilosophie Schellings: Ein Beitrag zur Kritik des Hegelschen Systems* (Vienna and Munich: R. Oldenbourg, 1965), 68ff., 97, 103, 107ff. Oeser has done the service above all of working out the late Schelling's Aristotelianism. At the time of the composition of Oeser's text, the following was not yet available: Hermann Schrödter, 'Die Grundlagen der Lehre Schellings von den Potenzen in seiner "Reinrationalen Philosophie"', *Zeitschrift für philosophische Forschung*, 40, no. 4 (1986), 562–85. Schrödter sees with great clarity the posited correlation between Kant's theory of the transcendental ideal and Schelling's approach.
79. [SW I/8, 214; *Ages* 8.]
80. *Weltalter* (Draft II), 129 [*Ages 1813*, 130].
81. ['Key' – tr.]
82. [SW II/1, 585–6. This is from the address, *Über die Quelle der ewigen Wahrheiten*, *On the Source of Eternal Truths* (hereafter *Sources*), given towards the end of Schelling's career and life.]
83. [SW II/1, 585.]
84. [SW II/1, 283 n.1.]
85. [This disparaging remark regarding Schelling is from Ludwig Feuerbach's *Das Wesen des Christentums*, which first appeared in 1841. Allesandro Cagliostro (1743–95) was an infamous forger and swindler who trucked in the 'occult' arts.]
86. Schelling, *Grundlegung der positiven Philosophie*: Münchener Vorlesung WS 1832/33 und SS 1833, ed. Horst Fuhrmans (Turin: Bottega D'Erasmo, 1972), 222.
87. Ibid. [See also SW I/10, 144, trans. Andrew Bowie, *On the History of Modern Philosophy* (Cambridge: Cambridge University Press, 1993), 147 – tr.]

III.

Transition to a Reconstruction of *The Ages of the World*: Metaphysics and the Theory of Predication

Schelling's *The Ages of the World* is incontrovertibly a great experiment in metaphysical speculation, which has become, with the exceptions of Heidegger and Whitehead, alien to contemporary philosophy. Before turning to the text of *The Ages of the World*, it would therefore seem appropriate to secure a methodical sense of metaphysics. If such a recovery is to produce anything relevant, then naturally we need not enter into a historically oriented discussion of the metaphysical tradition, but should endeavour to develop an understanding of metaphysics that is to some extent indifferent to the tradition, but without disowning it.

The introduction of a methodical concept of metaphysics, constructed along three approaches, will bring us, without contriving it, into communication with certain contemporary philosophical arguments that are incompatible with it and must therefore be discussed.

Following this and from the concept of metaphysics thus achieved, I will develop the perspective in which the substantive issue that Kant had in view with his conception of the *transcendental ideal* can be addressed. For Schelling continues to seize on this conception in his lectures to the Berlin Academy of Sciences of 15 March and 29 April 1847, and again on 17 January 1850,[1] so as to develop it in the manner of a belated conceptual introduction to the variously formulated conceptual world of *The Ages of the World*.

With this, we have established the presuppositions for entering upon the reconstruction of *The Ages of the World*, which will aim to make some aspects of this project conceptually comprehensible as an articulable programme.

§ 8 Metaphysics and the conditions of successful predication

Metaphysics spells out the structure of the singular judgment (*Fa*) as the structure of the world. Twentieth-century analytic philosophy of language has shown how exacting a task this is, and has occasionally recommended that it be abandoned. Yet it turns out that we do not get free from metaphysics by avoiding it. It is better to pursue it in a manner that is justifiable according to the standards of contemporary philosophy. Or, more carefully and modestly: one should at least endeavour to articulate the concerns of metaphysics in accordance with these standards, and for present purposes I need no more than this to make my experiment.

First, we will explain the particular role of the singular judgement in order to mark out the methodical commitment of metaphysics. The particularity of its role consists simply in this, that judgements of the type 'this is so and so' (*Fa*) are indispensable information channels, points of intersection between sensibility and understanding. They stand for the manner in which we linguistically 'digest' observation, and so attest to the epistemic metabolism between world and mind. Without them, there would be no such thing as knowledge of the world.

Now if, with Wittgenstein, we start from the position that 'to understand a proposition means to know what is the case, if it is true',[2] we acquire a general understanding of such *Fa*-judgements concerning an analysis of their truth conditions. This analysis further includes, above all, a clarification of the modes of application of singular (*a*) and general (*F*) terms.

By means of singular terms (e.g., 'this here', 'the second from the right', etc.), we indicate a perceptible object in order to make it comprehensible as such-and-such to our interlocutor when we ascribe ('is') a predicate (e.g., 'dog', 'the perpetrator') to it. Predication therefore combines two functions: by means of singular terms we *indicate* a predicable object, and by ascribing predicates to it we *classify* the object.

Regarding the *conditions of application* of singular and general terms, which have been extensively researched[3] but will not further be explained here, the *conditions* under which their application is *felicitous* must be distinguished. These felicity conditions comprise presuppositions on the part of the speaker and on that of the world.

On the speaker's side, certain pre-linguistic competences must already be available for use so that a well-ordered application of terms of the same kind may be effected. We must therefore make use of an elementary, and certainly a pre-linguistic, discriminatory competence that enables us to distinguish both between and among optical, acoustic, tactile and olfactory occurrences as signals. We must also be able to distinguish between the situations, and their phases and segments, pertinent to these occurrences and signals from those occurrences and signals themselves. Moreover, this discriminatory competence has recourse to an essentially elementary, or certainly pre-linguistic, capacity for memory, which ensures that observed optical, acoustic, etc., 'impressions' are not extinguished immediately, and also that the corresponding situational impressions are retained and can be qualitatively identified across a pre-linguistic scale of similarities. Without these two elements of pre-linguistic competence, we would undoubtedly be in no position practically and successfully to practise the organised use of signs.[4] Anyone therefore who puts forward the thesis that all the structures of this world are exclusively to be construed as linguistic accomplishments[5] has at the very least failed to note these presuppositions for the successful and well-ordered use of signs.

Yet the proponent of this thesis overlooks one other aspect. For the conditions for the successful, regular use of signs, as comprising, on the speaker's side, the stated pre-linguistic capacities for distinction and memory, are moreover built into 'hypotheses' concerning the structure of the world, hypotheses that we do not as such 'assert' or 'deny', but that we subscribe to *when* we encounter linguistic distinctions or recall something similar. That is, the success of distinction and memory presupposes that the world presents *distinctions*, differences, and conversely, also a certain *uniformity*. That these 'hypotheses' are implied in every occurrence of distinction and recollection, respectively, means among other things that distinction and recollection as existing capacities are licensed products of the world and must for this reason be compatible with the structure of the world in itself. The compatibility, guaranteed by the contingent course of the world, between our epistemic achievements and the world does not imply a thesis of isomorphism, but simply the thesis that our distinctions and recollections can be corrected by the world. We need not at all determine or define the manner in which the epistemic metabolism between the world and knowledge takes place; we need not metaphorically require that something like a *reflection* takes place here. All that we need assume is that, however our 'image' of the world is constructed, it at least possesses the property of being corrigible by that world. If this *corrective contact* is warranted, a minimal condition of adequacy has already been fulfilled, which is at least sufficient to explain how the process of learning is possible. And such processes of learning will be optimised, albeit not generated, by the practice of the well-ordered use of signs.

The well-ordered use of *singular* terms therefore already has recourse to the pre-linguistic capacity of *distinction*, just as the well-ordered use of *predicates* has recourse to the pre-linguistic capacity of *recognising similarities*. With these fragmentary considerations of the past of predication, of the 'structure of pre-predicative experience',[6] I am naturally not making any claim to completeness, nor do I need to. All I must guarantee is the general claim that the conditions of predicative success are referred to pre-linguistic competences, which imply, for their part, *modo operandi* hypotheses concerning the structure of the world.

Naturally, one can have different views regarding the status of the hypotheses (on the pluriformity and uniformity of the world) built into the elementary competences of recollection and differentiation that, indeed, the human being is.

If we interpret the proposition, 'It is the case that the structure of the world presents differences and uniformities', as the condition of success for linguistic capacities *a fortiori*, since they are already pre-linguistic capacities in the sense that these conditions must *sub specie* be satisfied by acts of discrimination and memory, insofar as these acts are to be possible at all, then we establish this proposition in the weak sense as a component of a *transcendental argument*.

If by contrast we are to interpret the proposition such that the so-called conditions of success must already be fulfilled as conditions that license the existence of acts of discrimination and recollection as such *a parti mundi*, then we establish this proposition in the strong sense as a component of an *ontological argument*, addressed to certain structures that the world *in itself* must possess.

Presumably both arguments are to be understood as compatible with each other, but as different answers to different formulations of the question.

Whether transcendental or ontological or both, however, it naturally cannot be ruled out that there is yet a fourth position that keeps the entire configuration of these status questions, these speculative inferences, from closing in on itself.

Nelson Goodman sought to justify such a position. He refers to the problem of induction. It was indeed early noted that the practice of inductive inference (from known to unknown cases) equally implies hypotheses concerning the structure of the world, such as, for example, a consistent course of worldly events, the justification of which causes difficulties, difficulties at any rate detrimental to the reputability of inductive practice. Goodman dislikes this entire strategy:

> I suppose that the problem of justifying induction has called forth as much fruitless discussion as has any half-way respectable problem of modern philosophy. The typical writer begins by insisting that some way of justifying predictions must be found; proceeds to argue that for this purpose we need some resounding universal [meaning: transcendental or ontological, W.H.] law of the Uniformity of Nature, and then inquires how this universal principle can itself be justified. At this point, if he is tired, he concludes that the principle must be accepted as an indispensable assumption; or if he is energetic and ingenious, he goes on to devise some subtle justification for it [e.g., a transcendental deduction or a constructive justification in the sense of the Erlangen school,[7] W.H.]. Such an invention, however, seldom satisfies anyone else; and the easier course of accepting an unsubstantiated and even dubious assumption much more sweeping than any actual predictions we make seems an odd and expensive way of justifying them.[8]

Goodman's arguments boil down to this recommendation: to inquire only into how exactly these inductive inferences function. For our purposes: how *Fa*-judgements can be made explicable by the regulative mechanisms of language alone. Whoever wants more must undertake something the results of which are at least far less compelling than any inductive inference, however insecure, or any *Fa* judgement, however fallible.

I believe that Goodman's argument, which I might call Ciceronian, is actually consistent. This means, however, only that no one may be constrained to any particular formulation of a question. Again, it is naturally and especially important for metaphysical questions, insofar as there are such questions at all, simply that they do not have anything to do with *natural* problems or problems concerned to ensure survival, but with *artificial* problems. Artificial problems of this kind are perhaps intellectually stimulating and have emancipatory effects – so, at least, certain philosophers assert – but they have no purpose connected in the strict sense to survival strategies. A concept of philosophical speculation of this kind is in any case nothing new, but rather strictly Aristotelian: metaphysics is not business as usual.[9]

Now, to return to our speculations, in the attainment of the pre-linguistic level, not only have we made a profit as regards an increase in the stock of phenomena, we have also made a loss: in any case, on this level it is not yet something like individual entities in the strict numerical sense that are indicated, nor properties in the sense of sharply defined extensions, classes and relations, that is, discrete attribution spaces. At this level, we have at best the more or less similar, in the individual as in the whole; in short, here we only have diffuse attribution spaces at our disposal. We do not have a quantifiable and invariant image of the world that, for example, requires the instruments of predicate calculus and supplied by identity, and that Gisbert Hasenjaeger has vividly called a *discrete ontology*.[10] All the mathematised sciences require this ontology. On the basis of this ontology, one requires no concept of things, resistants, objects or entities distinct from numbers. This characteristic of discrete ontology is clearly evident in the interpretation of the Löwenheim–Skolem theorem stemming from W. V. O. Quine:

> The narrowly logical structure of a theory – the structure reflected in quantification and truth functions – is insufficient to distinguish its objects from the positive integers.[11]

On the pre-linguistic level, however, we have not yet explicitly 'reflected' the instruments of propositional or predicate calculus, so neither can we here make use of the virtues of a discrete ontology. This means that we must relinquish any crystal-clear criterion of identity, and thus have an image of the world as impressive as it is expressive, but above all qualitatively interconnected, grounded in an essentially diffuse, *indiscrete* ontology. But only by way of a highly porous ontology such as this do we reach the dimension of the presuppositions of predication in which the processes of formation of univocity can be studied *in statu nascendi*. Only thus, in any case, can we throw open those hypotheses that ultimately enable reliable predication. And we have already mentioned by name two pale hypotheses of this kind, to the effect that the world shows in itself differences, similarities and a certain uniformity that, however we represent it, is in any case so constituted that it stands in corrective contact with our representational efforts. Now results of this type are not really surprising, and have equally therefore come to be understood, in the philosophy of linguistic analysis, as contributory to *descriptive metaphysics*, as by P. F. Strawson, for example;[12] or, although not without irony, as thoughts that may be counted as belonging to *transcendental metaphysics*, as by W. V. O. Quine.[13] Whether descriptive or transcendental, however, the philosophy of linguistic analysis flirts with metaphysics, and where it does not do this, it at least attempts to inherit its standing, insofar as it can be inherited in terms of linguistic analysis, as in Ernst Tugendhat's expressionist project of a formal semantics. It remains characteristic of all these conceptions that they never really abandon the grounds of discrete ontology, or at least view it as standard.

§ 9 Metaphysics and the adequacy conditions of predication

This orientation with regard to discrete ontology is certainly justified if one wants to discuss the ontological foundation of mathematicised natural sciences, which are geared overall to the *safeguarding of knowledge*. But this optic is already too narrow where one also wants to hold the ontology open for aspects of the *search for knowledge*. And that is advisable if the question, 'What can I know?', is to make a contribution to the question, 'What is the human?' This is to say: the epistemic dimension must not be anthropologically neutralised, and this is what happens if it is only discussed at the level of the safeguarding of knowledge. An anthropological deficit in epistemology is therefore unavoidable if the fundamental dimensions of the search for knowledge remain hidden beforehand for the whole epistemic corpus of every safeguarding of knowledge. For this fundamental character of searching also adds to the level of the safeguarding of knowledge through knowledge gained in its ultimately fallibilistic character and secured according to the strictest criteria. There also seems to be such an anthropological deficit in the exclusive orientation to discrete ontology in the analytic philosophy of language for certain stocks of problems, which sometimes appears stifling. Naturally, this orientation is *methodically* indispensable, but that is by no means the case *thematically*, but rather at the price of a reduction of the phenomenality of the *condition humaine*.

From this we can see that discrete ontology is essentially tailored for the declarative, *assertory* aspect of linguistic use, which invariably has a questioning and *problematic* 'advance from the rear' for its occasion. The elementary predication is always first of all construed as an answer. Indeed, more precisely because the (per a) indicative and (per F) classificatory double function of the Fa judgement is an answer to either a 'What is that?' question or a 'What does that mean?' question. The 'What is that?' question refers to the predicate for a given object: what applies to it? The 'What does that mean?' question refers, for a given predicate, to the objects on which the predicate can be exemplified.[14]

These oppositional directions of inquiry release search processes, which are defined through their termination in the establishment of a predicative structure. Predication is the assertory finale of such search processes. The structure of this search process is in general defined in the end-formula that Something whatever (*irgendetwas*) is Something whatever (Φx). Because the search processes are oriented towards a correct instantiation of Φ or of x, to a certain extent they run into the variable structure of predication, in order to fill in through a or F.

Such search processes, which, through variable oriented heuristic approaches, are assertory judgements, belong – according to the analysis of the felicity conditions of predication – likewise to the domain of metaphysics, if it is approached from the optic of the internal relationship of predication. In this optic, metaphysics analyses structures of universal search-fields, which have to be stable if we want to find something assertory in them. These structures establish the search directions through questions, which the variable 'Something whatever', the universal object of the search, establishes as what it has to be if it can be searched for at all.

We searchingly ask ourselves: what something is (τί ἐστι), how big (πόσον), how it is procured (ποιόν), where (ποῦ) and how it is (πρός τι), when (ποτέ) it is; we ask about its position (κεῖσθαι), what it has (ἔχειν), what it does (ποιεῖν), or how it reacts (πάσχειν). The ontological character of these Aristotelian categories[15] arises only from the perspective of searching for something-whatever; from the perspective of being confirmed as successful; that is, these categories have their mere semantic character from the perspective of assertoric conclusions.

Searching also produces objectivity where the finding can only be characterised semantically. An example of the type of objectivity that is to be expected within the cognitive search process is supplied by the venerable German term *Wesen*, essence. It has not received a good press in analytic philosophy of language circles; for some it does not belong to their licensed heritage because of its offensive provenance. Naturally, Quine pointed out its unflattering parentage: 'The Aristotelian notion of essence was the forerunner, no doubt, of the modern intension or meaning.'[16]

Nevertheless, I would here like to argue that even the concept of essence, and not just in terms of its reference, is indispensable admittedly *only* in a heuristic discourse. Here essence, as the essence of the matter, simply stands for the intuitive condition of adequation, for example our definitory attempts, our search for appropriate conceptuality, correct interpretation or explication. I consider, for example, how I can make a certain psychological nuance comprehensible to someone. I have also not yet articulated this phenomenon beforehand and have a hard time doing so, yet I know enough about it that I can reject with certainty interpretative suggestions, without already having provided a satisfactory interpretation. These rejections can in principle be introduced in this way: that (somehow) misses the essence of the matter, that does not hit the essence of the matter.

We express ourselves similarly if a suggested definition does not appear to be adequate. The essence of the matter is what we are oriented towards when we strive for adequation. The essence of the matter is the object of an intuitive orientation of knowing with which to search for an adequate explication. On the other hand, the essence is never what we put forth as a conclusive and factual assertion; it is not what the approved definition or explication supplies; it is not to be grasped as an assertion or proposition. There is no essential definition. Metaphysics in the style of essential definitions, therefore a nominal metaphysics, is not possible. Essence indeed directs our efforts to name, but the nominal net income is not a representation of the essence (otherwise these contributions would be effectively infallible). Accordingly, it is important to indicate this propositional incomprehensibility of the essence, because this circumstance makes it clear that the directive for the search for adequate predication is partly anchored in a domain that is indubitably neither predicative nor propositional. This naturally has as a consequence the expression of the feeling that, for example, a suggested definition that misses the essence of the matter is *not an argument*, but rather something like an *epistemic expression* in a heuristic discourse. But the epistemic justification of the expression of this feeling ultimately follows the fact that, *without recourse to this feeling, we could not continue to be critical when there is no other argument available to us.*

In this manner, the essence also has an indispensable critical function. In a heuristic discourse, we are inevitably essentialists, something that we are in no case allowed to be at an assertory level. But heuristic essentialism and assertory fallibilism are just as compatible with another as methodic dogmatism and theoretical criticism.

By this critical limitation and the establishment of metaphysics exclusively in heuristic discourse, we can nonetheless say that the object of metaphysics is the essence of the world. And the essence of the world is the enigma of the world, or

> 'was die Welt
> Im Innersten zusammenhält'
> [The inmost force
> That bonds the very universe][17]

§ 10 Metaphysics and the existential conditions of predication

It is already obvious on systematic grounds that it is necessary to make the formulation of metaphysical questions comprehensible not only from the internal relations of predication, that is, via an analysis of their felicity conditions and their adequation conditions, but – if we might put it with such beautiful unclarity – in order to grasp 'the whole', also from the external relations of predication.

To achieve this, we will construct an argument that could be called the Wittgensteinian-Schelling Argument. It has the following structure:

0. There is only one world
1. The world is everything that is the case
2. What is the case is a property of the world
3. It is the case that there is knowledge of the world

It follows from this that:

4. The world has the property that there is knowledge of the world

Which can also be expressed as:

5. The world knows itself

The reflexivity ('knows itself') in (5) naturally cannot be obtained from (4), but – logically considered – only inferred, and indeed only insofar as one mistakes the two appearances of the expression 'world' in (4) as suggesting reflexivity.

Naturally there are only some entities in the world that can know themselves and other worldly entities, but – and this is the half-way legitimising intuition for (5) – these entities are worldly products, so that one must read (5) more exactly thus: the world knows itself by way of some of its products. Differently again: the world has among all its properties *one* in consequence of which it knows itself. And this can, after the manner of an anthropic principle, also be expressed thus: the world has among other things an *auto-epistemic structure*. And we may add to this: other worldly properties must be logically compatible with this structure. Thus the proposition,

'The world has an auto-epistemic structure *and* the world has *x* structures (other structures)', cannot always be false.

Over and above this, other worldly structures must be so constituted that they are not only logically compatible with the auto-epistemic structure, but since we have presupposed that there is only one world, they must also be ontically compatible with it, that is, they must stand in some kind of similarity relation. This is requisite because other structures must at least also be so constituted that they permit the auto-epistemic structure to arise, and that conversely, moreover, must also be somehow graspable from the latter. From this point of view, other worldly properties also evince, *ceteris paribus*, an auto-epistemic structure. The epistemic structure of the other worldly properties is earlier, according to their existence, than the auto-epistemic structure of the world, but later according to the concept. It belongs therefore equally to the past of the auto-epistemic structure as to its present, although not necessarily to its future.

To this extent, we may say that the world's process, with the transition from epistemic structures to the auto-epistemic structure of the world, demonstrates an historical aspect, with which the remaining history of the world must in turn be compatible. This is, however, then the case when the history of the universe is *also* the history of its self-knowledge. That means that the history of the universe as a whole, not only of biological life,[18] can also be understood as a knowledge-acquisition process.

Now this entire sequence of thoughts appears initially plausible, but towards the end and particularly with a view to consequences not yet drawn from it, bizarre. It implies, for example, this thesis: the 'knowing subject' is not really the human, but rather the universe. We are only derivatively that subject as organs of an obscure universal subject: I think, therefore it thinks (*cogito ergo cogitat*).[19] However, with this obscure universal subject we have approximately attained to the intuition that motivated Schelling's metaphorical application of *The Worldsoul* (1798). By this expression we should as a first approximation perhaps think no more than something like the potential for a self-organising universe with an auto-epistemic structure.

And if we are ultimately bound to anchor this epistemic structure in the elementary structure of predication, and consequently also to grasp the auto-epistemic structure of the universe as essentially predicative, then we must also construe the history of the universe after the model of an *a priori* self-enlarging judgement,[20] that is, as a kind of synthetic *a priori* judgement. Schelling formulates the maxim of construction thus: 'Not therefore that **we know** nature as *a priori*, but nature **is** *a priori*.'[21]

Certainly, how this is to function is itself still unclear if, pursuing this image, we ask: how is the beginning of this *a priori* self-enlarging universe to be grasped? Doesn't the auto-epistemic structure necessarily have ontic presuppositions that fundamentally cannot be made epistemically comprehensible? For from what does the beginning of the auto-epistemic process draw its energy? If not the *entire* panorama, then *this* point at least remains obscure: and we will see that its illumination is an essential preoccupation of Schelling's, more specifically, of the first book of *The Ages of the World*.

Yet there is another problematic consequence of the entire sequence of thoughts. It implies a teleological thesis, namely, that the explicit self-knowledge of the universe in our heads holds a privileged status in its history, a status from which – recurrently – this history inevitably acquires an epistemic *façon d'être* in the sense of a 'self-referential cosmogony' *à la* John Wheeler.[22] As plausible as at first it seems that the world that has produced a knowing being must be thought such that the productive forces must after all be capable of such a result, it is nevertheless just as problematic that these forces should be of the same kind as what they have produced. For obviously there would here be a reference to emergent results, to consequences that cannot be reductively explained, that is, to the emergence of completely new systemic properties.

An imaginary Schelling, defending the foregoing conception, would certainly reply to this that the emergence of completely new systemic properties neither can nor should be contested, but this only implies that the process of the universe must be understood as a creative process, and if this is so, then inevitably we measure it according to the one kind of creativity known to us, namely exactly that of which we, as epistemic beings, are capable in art and science.

The project here sketched is therefore quite compatible with the emergence of completely new systemic properties, indeed this emergence can to a certain extent be claimed as evidence for the adequacy of the outline and its epistemic tailoring: the inventiveness of the universe is reasserted in our epistemic constitution and recurrently becomes comprehensible through it.

The opponent of this metaphysics would certainly follow up and ask: why should we take the universe to be just as the temporally limited existence of knowing beings prescribes? Why should our understanding of the universe be measured against exactly the epistemic constitution of the one thing in the world of which we know that it has arisen and will perish again, unless the universe must particularly suffer from this passing?

In brief: are we not precisely compelled by the insight into the finitude of the species *homo sapiens* to set out an image of the world that is completely independent of the ephemeral existence of epistemically competent beings?

An imaginary Schelling, defending the metaphysics here sketched, would reply to this that this objection is ambiguous. If it states that we are to make ourselves a strictly neutral epistemic image of the universe, then the objection would be immediately self-refuting: a knowledge-neutral 'image' of the universe is naturally no longer an 'image' at all. If the objection only states that in sketching the universe we must take account of the circumstance that this universe is independent of *our* knowing, that our knowing does not produce the universe, then this requirement only forces its way through an open door, since this theory in consequence certainly does not produce *our* knowledge of the universe, but conversely, the universe produces our knowledge. This is precisely a consequence of the auto-epistemic structure of the universe that this theory postulates.

The objection could finally be read such that the universe must be constituted in this sense independently of its knowing, as knowing qua *Fa* judgements of a fundamentally propositional kind, and thus there are 'that *p*' events that, as atemporal phenomena, have a validity of a fundamentally different ontological status than do the temporal phenomena of the thingly, the factical, and genesis. An imaginary Schelling would respond to this that the distinction between genesis and validity must of course be taken into account, but must this be done by such an expensive and ultimately implausible theory as an (internal) two-worlds theory that merely extrapolates the designated antithesis by establishing a *mundus intelligibilis* and *mundus sensibilis*? Shouldn't we, on the basis of ontological parsimony, endeavour to make this undoubtedly important antithesis compatible with the essentially more plausible theory of *one* world, *one* universe? Of a world, therefore, that must be so constituted that it is capable of such an antithesis between spatiotemporal and propositional things?

Now, such counter-questions are certainly not already the solution to the problem urged, but perhaps they make us aware that one alternative to Schelling's (internally) monistic metaphysics is, on this footing, just another, namely, a dualistic metaphysics. The problem is certainly delicate: validity phenomena of the propositional kind, which may be true or false, are certainly to be strictly separated from what is spatiotemporally the case. But how strictly? Are there absolutely no points of comparison? Günther Patzig has proposed in this connection an instructive analogy as an aid to understanding the concept of validity in the truth-conditions of a proposition:

> We may immediately decide to hear the expression 'truth conditions' as far as possible as we hear the expression 'living conditions'. Just as an organism can only live in an environment that fulfills its living conditions, and immediately dies when these living conditions are essentially altered, so a proposition can only be true as long as its truth conditions are fulfilled.[23]

Naturally, this analogy has its limits. These are essentially set

> [in] that the property of the truth of propositions is not a comparatively real property of these propositions, as of course the property of being alive can be a real characteristic of organisms. A true proposition is not distinguished from a false proposition as a living from a dead organism. The change from 'true' to 'false' is not a temporal transition like that from life to death.[24]

As little as this distinction can be denied, the analogy nevertheless makes a structural continuity clear that is secured by maintaining the distinction. Stated otherwise: that we can produce no greater clarity concerning the manner of the universe's natural cognitive process than by factically acknowledging the world should trouble us no more than the circumstance that this is also true in the same way of our own cognitive processes. Thus we copiously simulate the structure of natural processes, as well as our own cognitive processes (artificial intelligence), through algorithms. In any case, we also know that the simulation of our cognitive processes (perhaps of natural processes, too) is in principle incomplete and in this sense probably also inadequate.

For presupposing that an algorithm is a specific type of calculation, then it is already true of such a comparatively simple concept as that of the 'finite' that we may indeed prove that all its specifications are equivalent, but that it is thereby also proven that there is no calculation that achieves this. Hasenjaeger formulated this result, from Mostowski, thusly: 'No codifiable system of deductive possibilities exhausts the content of the intuitive concept of finitude.'[25] It has also been put thus, that there is no axiom of finitude.[26] This means that essential aspects of our cognitive achievements cannot be simulated by algorithms. So too, we can know the universe only as far as we can know ourselves, and conversely, the extent to which we can know ourselves is also the extent to which the universe knows itself.

It must additionally be noted that the theory of a knowledge-achieving universe is oblique with respect to the disjunction materialist or idealist. It is idealist, since material processes will also be understood as natural cognitive processes; but it is equally materialist, since the theory implies the thesis that our knowledge is simply the document and organ of the manner in which the world knows itself.

Nor equally will this theory make the antithesis between propositional and material processes simply disappear. It consists exclusively in this, that in some fundamental sense, compatibility conditions between these entities must be fulfilled internally in the world. So this conception is incompatible with an inner-worldly entity dualism. Namely, such a dualism has to do with the insuperable problem of transfer between the two domains of entities. If this dualism managed to resolve this problem in a satisfactory way, it would at that moment cancel itself.

Finally, for an inner-worldly monism, this option is thoroughly compatible with an outer-worldly dualism. This is because inner-worldly monism is ontologically tailored: the compatibility conditions between spatiotemporal and propositional entities are postulated as fulfilled. By contrast, outer-worldly dualism is ontically tailored: the energies for there being something at all are irreducible without remainder to entities that can be predicatively characterised. This 'remainder' meaning of being is therefore only accessible via pre-predicative experience, which in consequence will acquire 'currency' only outside the semantic dimension. The ultimate character of this experience does not remove the epistemic monism of the universe, but drives us before the universe, into pre-worldly zones.

Schelling insists emphatically on this outer-worldly dualism, and he equally insists that this does not cancel inner-worldly monism, but remains its operating presupposition, which threatens to blow up the entire predicative corpus.

It is, of course, clear that the speculative character of this universal, internal holism, with pre-worldly presuppositions ensuring that it remains compatible with outer-worldly dualism, cannot be denied. But all the alternatives with comparable claims also have such a speculative status. Certainly those among all the alternatives with the greatest plausible yield will be shown preference. But we will have to learn this on the outlined route to Schelling. For *ex ignotis non eligendum est* [choice does not issue from the unknown].

§ 11 Starting conditions of predication: Kant's theory of the transcendental ideal

We have thus far been concerned with guidelines for a methodological metaphysics, in approximate rather than compulsive alignment with Schelling. These lines draw on the aspect of the *felicity conditions* of predication based on ontological hypotheses about the structure of the world; on the aspects of the *production conditions* and *adequation conditions* of predication based on categories and the concept of essence; and finally on the aspect of the *existential conditions* of predication based on the bizarre idea of – admittedly not without presuppositions – an auto-epistemic universe. It is clear that traditional philosophical projects flicker through these three operations of methodological metaphysics, but due to our methodical orientation towards predication, we remain at the same time at a sufficient remove from them to be able to connect to contemporary philosophy. It might be all the more surprising that these preliminaries are no detour *en route* to Schelling, because the passage based on one of Kant's theories, in which we want for the first time to take him at his word, presents metaphysics exactly as we have thus far methodically sketched it, based in part on the theory of predication. And indeed, the textbook example of this is the *transcendental ideal* in the *Critique of Pure Reason*.[27]

Kant first introduces here what he calls the *principle of determinability*. This principle can be more precisely understood as the *principle of the further determination of predicates* and means that each given predicate *F* can invariably only be further determined through one of two mutually contradictory predicates, *G* and *Ḡ*, so as not to violate the principle of contradiction, *(x) ¬ (∃x) (Gx ∧ Ḡx)*. This principle of the further determination of predicates therefore merely has the status of a limitation of any continuation of predication only based on logical grounds. It can be formulated thus with running predicates *x*: *(x) (Fx → Gx ∨ Ḡx)*. This is distinguished from what according to Kant is the *principle of continuous determination*, which does not deal with predicates but rather with the objects of predicates.

This principle can be understood as the *principle of the starting conditions* of predication. In a manner of speaking, I seek an appropriate predicate for a given *a*, so that not just the logical limitations with respect to the predicate hold that, of all *given* predicates *F*, only either every *F* or its contradictory opposite *F̄* can apply to it, otherwise it would violate the principle of the excluded middle, *(x) (Fx ∨ F̄x)*. But rather with regard to the object it is also true that for all *possible* predicates *F*, every *F*, or its contradictory opposite *F̄*, *must* apply to it.[28] This implies: objects of predication are thoroughly determined. The consummate knowledge of an object therefore has the form of an infinite conjunction: *Fa ∧ Ga ∧ ...* and this is the true section for *a* from the infinite alternation *Fx ∨ F̄x ∨ Gx ...* I call this infinite alternation the *Universal Register of predicates*. I also only seek a predicate *F* that is true for *a*, so I am already referring to this Universal Register. That is, in every predication the existence of this register is in fact acknowledged; it is presupposed by every start of predication. Kant grasped this Universal Register as the 'sum total [*Inbegriff*] of all predicates of things overall'. For this sum total of all predicates is simultaneously the whole leeway of possibility for objects of predication; the existence of the Universal Register is the condition of possibility for the objects of predication. Kant summarises:

> The proposition *Everything existing is thoroughly determined* signifies not only that of every given pair of opposed predicates, but also of every pair of possible predicates, one of them must always apply to it; through this proposition predicates are not merely compared logically with one another, but the thing itself is compared transcendentally with the sum total of all possible predicates. What it means is that in order to cognize a thing completely one has to cognize everything possible and determine the thing through it, whether affirmatively or negatively. Thoroughgoing determination is consequently a concept that we can never exhibit *in concreto* in its totality, and thus it is grounded on an idea which has its seat solely in reason, which prescribes to the understanding the rule of its complete use.[29]

This train of thought is so far unproblematic and can also be understood as a thought-experiment at the ground of discrete ontology. In fact, Gisbert Hasenjaeger conceived a World Catalogue that is compatible with Kant's Universal Register that he introduces in this way:

> A world with the structure described through discrete ontology would be perfectly determined through an – infinite, if need be – Catalogue C, of all the cases in which a quality is realised (that is, applies to a thing) and in which a relationship exists (that is, between a pair of things, a trio of things, etc.).[30]

Of course, such a Catalogue is practically unserviceable. Not only because signs for all things, qualities and relations would have to be at hand, but also – and this also goes for Kant's Universal Register – because each time, in order to determine whether a certain thing *a* does not have a certain quality *F*, one would have to go through the whole Catalogue 'and would, if need be, first get the answer "after an infinite number of steps", that is, not at all'.[31] Hasenjaeger finally introduces the Partial Catalogue C_A, which provides the truth interpretations for C_2. But since this is anyway only about a thought-experiment in which we might count on an ideal Catalogue-Author and Catalogue-Interpreter, we should not bother ourselves further with the practical problems of such a World Catalogue. It is only important for us that Kant's idea of a Universal Register, *to the extent that we have followed his considerations so far*, is nothing that could be discussed, for example, in the domain of his transcendental philosophy. The compatibility demonstrated here with discrete ontology, however, is no longer given for the further considerations of predication.

Kant first proposes to sort and put the Universal Register of predicates in order. The sorting principle should be the idea of the sum total of all possibilities, which is bound to the Universal Register. To be able to use this idea at all in the intended function of a sorting principle, Kant engages in a *sly* shift of meaning. The expression 'sum total [*Inbegriff*]' can be understood as 'extensional', and then it simply means as much as 'multiplicity' and 'domain'. This understanding is sufficient so far and is the reason why the discussion of the Universal Register has been compatible with discrete ontology. But the expression 'sum total' can also be understood as '*intensional*', and it then designates a maximal degree of comparison for a matter. So, the sum total of 'horse', extensionally understood, is the *quantity* of all horses, but intensionally understood, it is the *specimen type* of the horse. Kant *now* applies the expression 'sum total of all possibility' in this intensional sense and hence in the sense of a maximal degree of comparison of the possible. Only in this understanding can the expression 'sum total of all possibility' function as the ordering principle of the Universal Register. The expression now stands for a norm that checks the predicates of the Universal Register to see if they are compatible with it or not. Predicates that are not compatible with the maximal degree of comparison of the possible are filtered out of the Universal Register, starting with all inconsistent and redundant predicates. All empirical predicates are then filtered out because they only stand for deficient modes of the possible and hence are likewise incompatible with the idea of the maximal degree of comparison of the possible. With this step, our Universal Register has now in one fell swoop so emptied itself that one hardly dares to ask which predicates are still retained. And yet: what predicate is at long last compatible with our *a priori* sorting principle, the maximal degree of comparison of the possible? Obviously only this principle itself. For the sum total of all possibility as the maximal degree of comparison of the possible does not tolerate any other degree of the possible besides itself. The Universal Register shrinks to a single concept. For the single remaining expression 'sum total of all possibility' in its intensional understanding as maximal degree of comparison of the possible is now also a *singular terminus*, and it applies to exactly one object.

Kant names this object the *ideal of pure reason*,[32] about which he says that it 'is the one single genuine ideal of which human reason is capable'.[33] It is important that this ideal first gives the principle of the thoroughgoing determination of things overall its necessary inner lining since it is the one object that is, so to speak, the proto-object of all objects of predication. Kant elucidates this ideal in this function thus:

> Thus, if the thoroughgoing determination in our reason is grounded on a transcendental substratum, which contains as it were the entire storehouse of material from which all possible predicates of things can be taken, then this substratum is nothing other than the idea of an All of reality (*omnitudo realitatis*).[34]

In this material function for all possible predicates of things, the transcendental ideal can be characterised in this way: there exists for everything (x) as that (y) that which is identical to each and thus ensures that everything exists: $(x)\,(\exists y)\,(x = y)$. Hence the transcendental ideal in every predication that is addressed but never pronounced is the comprehensive object of *all* predications, and as such 'the concept of a *thing in itself*'.[35] The ideal is hence

> the original image (*prototypon*) of all things, which all together, as defective copies (*ectypa*), take from it the matter for their possibility, and yet although they approach more or less nearly to it, they always fall infinitely short of reaching it.[36]

In the end, this anthemic finding also motivates characterisations of the transcendental ideal such as 'original being (*Urwesen, ens originarium*)', 'highest being (*ens summum*)', 'being of all beings (*ens entium*)'.[37] Nevertheless this only deals with a hypostasised idea as the presupposition of the objects of predication, and hence we are left 'as to the existence of a being of such preeminent excellence in complete ignorance'.[38] It should surprise no one that we are left with this critical finding a hair's breadth away from a theologically relevant result. It will be all the more shocking when I say that one can reduce the whole discussion of the transcendental ideal to one half of the description of the function of *intentional variables* (not the variables in calculus) or intentional pronouns ('Something whatever'), that stands for what the search vector of all our epistemic efforts is directed towards. The transcendental ideal is simply what 'Something whatever' means, or, as Frege says, what the variable *x* indeterminately indicates. What is here indeterminately indicated is something obscure like the sum total of all objects. The complete understanding of the sign *x*, even before its instantiation through arguments, implies what Kant calls a *transcendental affirmation*, 'which is a Something [*Etwas*], the concept of which in itself already expresses a being, and hence it is called reality (thinghood [*Sachheit*]), because through it alone, and only so far as it reaches, are objects Something (things)'.[39]

It also seems that the idea of the thoroughgoing determination of a thing is something that can be connected in a more unconstrained way to the understanding of variables than anything else. For when we say that we are referring to Something whatever, we in fact refer, by virtue of semantic indetermination, to *everything to which we can specifically refer*, and we also refer to *everything that can be Something whatever*. We actually do not have to let an extensive understanding guide us here. For the expression 'everything that can be Something whatever' does not only have an aspect of multiplicity, but also an intensive aspect. We do not just refer, for example, to all horses, but also to all species in which something is a horse, from nags to the most noble Arabian horse. Variables stand for all things, for everything that can be a thing and, for each species, *how* it can be.

Now, an objection could be made: such a diffuse concept of everything that is on a sub-numerical level has such a 'fringy' meaning that, among other things, the homogeneity of this obscure 'object' is lost. Yes, one could suspect that this diffusion ultimately prevents us from being able to speak at all of *an* 'object'. However, semantic diffusion is not in principle tangential to the formal homogeneity of 'what is meant'. No matter how vague the terms, even those whose meaning one could hardly or not at all indicate (i.e., not knowing the rules of application), one is still referring to one thing[40] because each application of linguistic terms is already dependent on a fundamental orientation of our mental activities towards Something whatever (the intentional vector that is calibrated to the magnetic pole of the desired Something). So, Aristotle could quite rightly say: even the indefinite, the indeterminate, somehow designates Something (ἓν γάρ πως σημαίνει ... ἀόριστον).[41] If this were not the case, we could not speak about obscure things at all. What we refer to *by natural variables* is therefore our *One and All*. In a broad sense, it is that out of which everything is. In itself it has no contours, but it can take on all contours. In itself it is indifferent concerning singular and general terms. What we are overall referring to is *Something whatever that is Something whatever*. This provocative generic term for all objects of predication is, per undetermined existential-presupposition,[42] built into the mechanism of our already sub-semantic referential competence (attentional/intentional attitude):[43] *(∃x) (Φx)*. *Sub specie praedicationis* [under the aspect of predication], this proto-thing is what can be everything in every species: *the predicative protoplasm*. *Sub specie existentiae* [under the aspect of existence], from the perspective of the external relations of predication, it is that which has already come before everything that exists, and therefore related to what can be, is not, and yet related to what can be something at all (what is not yet), yet already was (existed): *the ontic past of the existing* (after the ancient linguistic usage: τὸ τί ἦν εἶναι *par excellence*). In this perspective, Kant's transcendental obtains the character of a *most ancient being*.

§ 12 Schelling's engagement with Kant's transcendental ideal

From the outset Schelling says that it is Kant's merit to have grasped the ideal so that it is first a single object, and that as such it 'contains at the same time the *material*, the *matter* of all possible and actual being'.[44] He reads the text of Kant's theory extraordinarily closely and maintains Kant's critical insight, that concerning the existence of this object we can do nothing by way of pure reason. We must briefly elucidate this critical perspective. In general, we test whether something exists by inquiring as to whether something actual can be encountered that fulfils the conditions by which something belongs to a manifold and the conditions by which it is the instantiation of a predicate. Given an explicable predicate such as 'snowman', for example, one begins an expedition to the Himalayas to see whether there is something of which this predicate holds true. Without such expeditions, that is, realised research procedures, guided by extensionally indeterminate and intensionally partly determinate predicates, nothing can be decided concerning existence. That something exists then means just that the extension of a predicate is not empty, there is an x of which F is valid. We have encountered an a that is F and say, in consequence: $Fa \rightarrow (\exists x)(Fx)$.

Now, since Kant's transcendental ideal is not something of which one F is said, but rather of which all Fs are said, and thus Φ is not something that is referred to as an a, but as all a's, that is, by x, it is clear that concerning such an object nothing can be decided as to its existence, since it is indifferent with respect to all particular, singular terms and predicates. Neither are we equipped with a *specification of something* (a determinate predicate) nor with a specific *research domain* (a determinate singular term, an identification) for an expedition. Thus Kant introduces the expression 'the sum total of all possibilities', as we have seen, precisely as a singular term, the formal property of which is to signify a particular object; but to ascertain the existence of this object, we are not equipped with what is standardly required for this ascertaining.

Schelling, naturally, sees this too. Thus, according to him, 'the mere "sum total of all possibilities" remains far too broad a concept even to allow us to attain something determinate'.[45] To first clarify the concept of the possible, he proposes 'to take actually existing things as the correlates of these possibilities, and to explain the possibility of their being those diverse kinds that they express in themselves [...]'.[46] Here Schelling restricts the concept of the possible to the scope of spatiotemporal existence, examples of which he gives as 'the inorganic', 'the organic', or more specifically, 'plant' and 'animal'. But all these diverse actualised possibilities of spatiotemporal existence naturally do not correspond to something like a 'sum total of all possibilities'. Perhaps this consideration might contribute to understanding such a 'sum total': that for all the so-called possibilities of spatiotemporal existence that there certainly are, they are not original, that is, they are created out of a merely presupposed possibility. Schelling in fact advocates this strictly evolutionary argument in order to advance into the depths included in the sum total of possibility:

Yet who does not sense that existing species cannot possibly be original? Rather, it is to be assumed that the species given in experience have always in the end been derived, by way of whatever intermediary links, from original differences that, hardly accidental, belong instead to the very nature of beings.[47]

Thus, by an evolutionary argument, Schelling seeks to grasp the sum total of all possibilities, which Kant took as the maximal degree of comparison for the possible, as the sum total of a *final* possibility, as the content of an *original* possibility. As a result, certainly both limit-concepts are equivalent, but are opposed to one another by different modes of access as the *highest being* and the *primal being*, as *ens summum* and *ens originarium*. Kant had already stated these distinct aspects of the one thing, although he did not introduce the *ens originarium* via an evolutionary argument, but rather through a geometrical one: just as all figures are only different modes of limiting infinite space, so 'all manifoldness of things is only so many different ways of limiting the concept of the highest reality, which is their common substratum'.[48] Schelling calls this a 'mechanical explanation by limitation'.[49]

Nevertheless, Schelling arrives at the totality of all possibility by reversion to a primal modality that gave all spatiotemporally realised possibilities their first, evolutionary opportunities. The question is, naturally, what can be determined concerning these primal modalities if they first make all spatiotemporal existence effectively possible? Before answering this question, we shall briefly explore the legitimacy of this evolutionary formulation of the question. Schelling does not understand this as the question of organic genesis alone, but 'extends' the dimensions of the question downwards, such that at issue is the genesis of the entire universe. The radical character of this extension is nothing problematic in and of itself, and is, in principle, quite consistent, especially if it is accepted that we will not be able to progress beyond certain limits in the scope of the question by means of, for example, empirical cosmology. But since it is unknown whether any of the historically given limits can be 'undermined' from below by new discoveries and theories, the speculative advance of the question in all its dimensions cannot assume any given state of cosmology or astrophysics, for instance, as premises; that is, speculative cosmology must proceed by a methodology *independent* of these empirical sciences. There might well be structural homologies that indicate that the same conceptual energies are operative in empirical and in speculative work. Further, that metaphysical speculation is nothing other than a fundamental heuristic that grounds every context of discovery and, to this extent, leaves a formal legacy for every process of theory formation. The only question is this: is there really a methodological procedure that guarantees the independence of speculative from empirical cosmology?

We have in the meantime prepared well for this question. There is indeed a methodological procedure, namely the 'downward' extension of the theory of predication as the exhaustion of the formal cosmological option of every predication. And if, with this assurance, we now turn back to Schelling to see how he answers the question of what can be said of the primal modality that in fact makes that which is everything spatiotemporal effectively possible, we will see that he orients his answer precisely by making recourse to the theory of predication, and it need not disturb us that this theory was still bound up, in his time, with the subject–object structure of judgement. The entire speculation for which Schelling strives as formal cosmology, or indeed theogony, can solely and exclusively be understood as the methodical development of the theory of predication, unless we really want to get bogged down with this.

Primal modality is first simply that which supplies the possibility of something in the sense of singular terms or predicates. Differently stated: the genesis of the universe is *sub specie predicationis* the process by which structures arise in such a manner that singular terms and predicates can be 'grasped'; that is, individuals that have properties and have relations. We have no concept of these entities other than the rules for the application of our terms, but these rules assume a universe with which they are compatible. Yet no such universe descends from heaven but is *sub species existentiae* the realisation of a possibility which we may infer using the guideline of the formal structure of the incomplete predicate Fx. Hence the genesis of the universe has the formal structure: what was always x and Φ has become Fa. Or, put differently: what was always some individual and some property (relation) has become individual with property (relation). If elementary predication is in fact the nucleus of our epistemic competence, then this thought-experiment rests essentially on a nuclear fission, that is, in the splitting of the predicative atom. The radiation (keeping with the image) thus liberated is in every case fatal for all discourse: it amounts to an uncontrolled dissipation of nonsense (*Unsinn*). For before an *Fx* structure is realised, what we understand by *x* and *F* is absolutely undiscoverable. The only content we have is that the subatomic elements of the split predicative atom must be considered as representing the possibility of a fusion into the elementary structure of meaning *Fx*. And Schelling pursues this strategy in precisely this sense, and this is exactly his characterisation of primal modality. That he thus exposes himself to the radiation of meaninglessness means primarily and only that he must explode the semantic dimension in order that its genesis become comprehensible. And one must indeed expose oneself to this risk if one wishes to attempt an answer to Schelling's already cited questions: 'Why is there meaning at all, why not meaninglessness instead of meaning?' and 'The entire world lies, as it were, caught in the nets of reason, but the question is, how did it come to be in these nets?'[50]

The transformation Schelling thereby effects consequently upon Kant's theory of the transcendental ideal, by interpreting that ideal as the singular reality that first allows the space of predicative possibility to be and thus meaning to arise, is, historically considered, a compact between Kant and Aristotle.[51] For what Schelling requires in the subatomic domain of predication is a theory of dissociated predicative elements, which is supplied by Aristotelian substance metaphysics, and a theory of possibility that contains a potential for becoming actual, which lies in Aristotelian dynamics. One certainly cannot say that, with this, Schelling merely executes a return to pre-Kantian metaphysics. What happens here is rather a connection with Aristotle, in order to indemnify the ontic deficit of Kant's transcendental philosophy. No one can be astonished that this thought-provoking crossing of Kantian and Aristotelian motifs exhibits, historically considered, a dubious, illegitimate lineage. On the other hand, however, this crossing is naturally in the spirit of Schelling, so that, systematically considered, we must perhaps consider it the birth of a new species.

§ 13 Towards a theory of predicative elementary particles

Immediately following his presentation of Kant's theory of the transcendental ideal, Schelling leads the reader to the laboratory to convince them, so to speak, experimentally of his thesis that this ideal is capable of an ontic deepening that Kant could not see. This is a deepening that consequently reckons with a prime possibility of every being, which itself must still exist as such if the genesis of the universe is not going to be a fiction. We have seen that this prime possibility is simply the presupposition for any *Fa* judgement, respectively or more precisely: the ontic presupposition for the creation of a universe that is compatible with such judgements. The first possibility in this sense is what was already there before Something whatever spatiotemporally exists. What already was before Something whatever spatiotemporally exists is Something whatever of which we otherwise know no predicate, nothing. Schelling calls this *x* 'the simple and pure subject of being'.[52] Something whatever to be is hence precisely 'what is first possible for beings'.[53] Because, whatever further determinations through predicates are being considered, predicates formally presuppose Something whatever, a pronominal being, to which they can be appropriate. Schelling immediately admits that Something whatever certainly does not exist in the sense that one says of a certain *x* that *Fx* is, that it exists as *(∃x) (Fx)*. One can therefore not assert that Something whatever exists, as Schelling expresses himself, 'in the declarative sense', since Something whatever is still grasped without predicates in that it is, according to Schelling's Aristotelian phrase, 'posited with privation'.[54] But this just means: Something whatever exists not in 'a certain *kind* of being', but not not at all (*nicht überhaupt nicht*).

We can here give each other an aid to understanding with an unsatisfactory predicative existence schema: *(∃x) (. . . x . . .)*. Schelling would also like to distinguish terminologically this wan and indifferent way in which Something whatever exists, the colourless pronominal being, from a certain way of existing in which predicates are grasped declaratively, that is, from predicative being. According to this, pronominal being is being 'simply having being [*bloß wesende*]' in distinction to any kind of predicative being. One could also put Schelling's point this way: Something whatever exists 'primordially', while it exists 'objectively' when it is predicatively determined. Finally, Something whatever exists, as it were, 'nakedly'. It is simply 'what has its own being [*sich-seyend*]', while predicative being, considered in isolation, is 'external to what has its own being'. In summary one can therefore say that Something whatever does not predicatively exist, but one cannot say that it does not exist at all. In view of Something whatever not existing predicatively, Something whatever is, as Schelling says in Greek, taking up a distinction from Plutarch, a μὴ ὄν, but that does not mean that it is therefore also an οὐκ ὄν, that is, that it does not exist at all. Not being of a certain species (μὴ εἶναι) and not being at all (οὐκ εἶναι) are not the same. 'The simple privation of being does not exclude being able to be [*seynkönnen*].' In this sense, Schelling grasps the indifferent 'kind of existence' of Something whatever as also as pure Being Capable [*Können*], as 'a potency of a being'. Something whatever purely exists as something that can be predicatively determined. In order to make the predicative privation of Something whatever, being *without predicates*, recognisable, Schelling deploys the symbol **–A**; to illustrate the 'declarative', that is, predicatively determined but *subjectless* kind of being, he deploys **+A**. Clearly neither can be for themselves without there consequently being nothing at all. Something whatever is precisely that with which we have to start, but it is clearly not yet what we want, 'for we want what the being is in *every* sense'.[55] Nevertheless: 'we cannot therefore throw that [= 'Something whatever', W.H.] away, because we would have to keep starting over; nothing whatsoever can be put before it in thinking, it is simply what is first thinkable (*primum cogitabile*)'.

We can always only *first of all* thematise that Something whatever without predicates and *then* subjectless predicative determination. And we nevertheless thereby first of all have only obtained two possibilities, potencies or 'moments of the being'. These are the fission products of the predicative core, that are simply in *one* sense, while simultaneously *not* the other. This contradiction has its resolution outside of itself, and this unity of both is for itself a Third, in which pronominal and predicative being can fuse. There is really no more room for this Third, however, if x and F are understood by themselves. In any case, it cannot be Something whatever and yet a predicate. But since one cannot see what else could be, and because 'there is no other opposition in relation to being', the Third must somehow be related to both.

What Schelling postulates here only makes sense if we grasp the Third as that ontic medium in which Something whatever *can* be a such-and-such, that is, as the possibility that Something whatever and predicative determination can stand together. The Third so understood is the ontic presupposition for the general proposition structure Φx, and hence for propositional being. But this also applies to this Third: 'because it cannot be what it is for itself, but only in community with others, we can only say of the Third (we want to designate it as ±**A**) [...] that it is a moment or a potency of the being'.[56] Compared to the simple being-itself of Something whatever (pronominal being) and the simple external-to-itself-being of predicative moments (predicative being), the Third (propositional being) is finally the one that is neither simply itself nor simply external to itself, but rather with itself: 'what possesses itself, what is powerful of itself'.[57] All three potencies, pronominal, predicative and propositional being together, now exhaust 'all possibility'.[58] All three moments of the being 'reciprocally [...] demand each other'.[59] All three moments are a presupposition of the establishment of the Φx structure. This structure is the placeholder for everything that can be the case, the leeway for the existence of facts. According to Schelling, it is 'an outline of the being, the simple figure or idea of the being, not itself'.[60]

In accordance with this characterisation, the Φx structure is also to be understood as a, to speak with Wittgenstein, 'projection of the possible state of affairs [*Sachlagen*]'.[61] But as simple projection, this threefold – through pronominal being, predicative being and propositional being – structured possibility does not yet receive a support; it circulates as simple possibility in itself. This projection requires an existential support, and we get this through the following thoughts. That the possible states of affairs exist depends on there being the Φx structure, and this by extension cannot be a possible state of affairs, but rather must actually be the case. This means the leeway of the possible state of affairs and fact defined by Φx, if it exists, not only trivially has a fact behind it (the fact that there is this leeway), but is also non-trivially, albeit obscurely, an event, or more precisely, an initial event. It happened that there is the leeway of the possible state of affairs. That this happened, again trivially, is a fact, but not again an event. Facts are metaphysically neutral, but events are not. But that first event, if it is the first, may not be temporal, although for the first event we can answer the question of when the event took place. It took place before time. If so, the first event naturally cannot be a cause in the physical sense and cannot even be characterised in a physical manner at all. This means: that something exists at all is not a physical event! We have thereby epistemically already lost the ground under our feet. But this loss is just a *sui generis* experience. According to Schelling it is the way pure positivity is given, that Something whatever exists at all. His argument here amounts to what I would like to name *orphic reference*: an explicit reference to pure positivity makes it disappear, although all oblique references (nominal identifications) are like Orpheus being followed by Eurydice. A verificatory position shatters on pure positivity. Verification here means liquidation. Where our conceptuality goes to its knees, the only thing that remains is the experience of ineffability as an attestation of the circumstance that something exists at all. This experience is, in a manner of speaking, an empirical criterion of the second degree. Put otherwise: *knowledge by acquaintance of boundless existence.*[62]

Regardless of what experiences we are capable of, that we have experiences as existing empirical beings implies an undetermined existential supposition that there is something at all. The first event is that Something whatever exists, not as this or that, but rather *ipso facto*, as pure manifestation. In retrospect, this results in our experimental arrangement in the following form:

i. we smash the atomic proposition,
ii. we specify both elementary particles, the pronominal Something whatever and the predicative what,
iii. we produce the conditions for their fusion, which leads to the establishment of the predicative structure Φx, and finally,
iv. we had to provide proof that there is this structure. Here we could not convey anything, except through the non-propositional experience that there is in fact Something whatever.

Schelling hence argues to the effect that regarding the 'simple matter of every particular possibility', should it exist, something must also exist 'about which it would be [*sic*]⁶³ said. This Something could not again be a mere possibility. This would have to be actuality in accordance with its nature; and this could therefore only be individual beings.'⁶⁴ This Aristotelian argument concludes from the form of the being to what is not itself formed, but rather a pure forming (*actus purus*). The leeway of possibility represented by *Φx* contains its own existence, not as possibility but rather as what preceded it as actuality. What precedes it, what is actual, is according to Schelling that 'Something or One' that 'demands the idea itself', that is therefore the 'cause of the being (αἴτιον τοῦ εἶναι)'⁶⁵ of the idea, of the *Φx* structure, and, insofar as it exists, of propositional being.

In principle, what Schelling here intends is the following: when we have pushed the theory of predicative elementary particles so far that they have again come to their fusion, we have therefore established the *Φx* structure. If we ask ourselves if this structure has a free-floating existence or another kind, then we would have to admit that we are basically asking about what can let the *Φx* structure be. It is that manifestation that guarantees the position of propositional being. The *Φx* structure as such does not guarantee any existence (Kant). Something has to correspond to it that simply *manifests itself*. Just such a thing is precisely what preceded the *Φx* structure and is the 'cause' of its being, and which otherwise is nothing. Without recourse to this position of pronominal being, the theory of predicative elementary particles is ultimately left hanging in mid-air. This means: the whole of cosmology and metaphysics is on the ground of predication theory. Of positional being, that is, what simply manifests itself in propositional being, one may say with Schelling that it is 'indeed determined by the idea [propositional being, W.H.]' and therefore distinguishable, 'but not by something that, independent of it, is actually a *thing*, of which Kant speaks, but which he could not provide'.⁶⁶ Schelling says that he first wanted to 'just *present* [*vorweisen*]' this thing that we are trying to comprehend as manifesting in propositional being, 'just as a thoughtworthy natural object must also be presented to those who did not know it before they can understand it'.⁶⁷ We have to content ourselves with Schelling's simple character of presentation in his analysis and pause briefly to see whether we are still in our senses or are already entangled in a speculation with stifling effects. So, we have to ask ourselves whether Schelling's speculation has a verifiable meaning or is suspiciously arbitrary. We have indeed tried to unfold the whole of his thought, as he himself urges, strictly from the theory of predication in order to interpret his so-called doctrine of potencies as a theory of *predicative existential components* [*Existentialien*]. But it still remains a question whether something is really gained thereby, especially since we finally came across a manifestation that has all three existential components (**−A**, **+A**, **±A**) *within* it, and so that they can thereby be, are *external* to themselves. Is this not just a play of metaphors that remains blind to the matter at hand? Certainly, one could say: regardless of what you develop from a theory of predication, at some point you will not be able to avoid manifestation. But what does this mean in a cosmological or cosmogonic sense? Should we not in the end abandon a halfway argumentative street paved with speculative discourse? We will see that we also cannot get rid of this question in the reconstruction of *The Ages of the World*, but we must not be insensitive either here or later to this difficulty. But for the time being, nothing more of this can be discerned.

With this presentation of the manifestation, Schelling now introduces the final considerations of his remarks on Kant's theory of the transcendental ideal. He once again retrospectively presents the whole enterprise that began with *Something whatever*, pronominal being, which is not supposed to be a *determinate* kind of being to which belongs *pure* Capacity [*Können*], the pure mightiness to be, and therefore a fully undetermined and sheer being, which is the beginning *par excellence*. With regard to Schelling's whole train of thought this means:

> It was a time when I could only imagine this sequence of possibilities of a for now future being in another way. But, as it seemed to me then and still seems to me now [1847], I dared to present a fully parallel sequence, and thereby established the principle: All beginnings lay in lack; the deepest potency to which everything is stitched is non-being, and this is the hunger for being.[68]

With these words, the old Schelling, on 29 April 1847 in the rudimentary lecture 'On Kant's Ideal of Pure Reason', refers to *The

Ages of the World, which he describes here as an *imagistic, but fully parallel* presentation of what we have gathered from his remarks. Schelling refers again to these 1847 remarks in his lecture, *On the Source of Eternal Truths*,[69] given before the Berlin Academy of Sciences on 17 January 1850, and affirms the given interpretation. There can therefore be no doubt that we already have in hand a key for understanding *The Ages of the World* and its vivid argumentation with Schelling's connection to Kant's theory of the transcendental ideal. Also, that Schelling incidentally refers one time to his small tract, *On the Deities of Samothrace*,[70] which he issued in 1815 as an addendum to *The Ages of the World*, even though the latter had not yet appeared, supports the thesis that we are here dealing with, so to speak, a delayed introduction to *The Ages of the World*. It is particularly suitable to prepare for an attempt to reconstruct this difficult work. And we will now – shuddering – embark on this attempt.

Notes

1. [See K. F. A. Schelling's Editor's Foreword to SW II/1, vi. Hogrebe is referring to the 11th and 12th lectures of Schelling's lecture series bearing the title *Einleitung in die Philosophie der Mythologie, Zweites Buch, Darstellung des rein rationalen Philosophie* (*Introduction to the Philosophy of Mythology, Second Book: Presentation of Pure Rational Philosophy*), SW II/1, 255–94, and to *Sources*, SW II/1, 575–90, with which he concluded that lecture series.]
2. Ludwig Wittgenstein, *Tractatus Logic-Philosophicus* [trans. C. K. Ogden (London: Routledge and Kegan Paul, 1981), hereafter *TLP*], 4.024.
3. See Ernst Tugendhat's *magnum opus*, *Vorlesungen zur Einführung in die sprachanalytische Philosophie* [*Introductory Lectures to the Analytic Philosophy of Language*] (Frankfurt am Main: Suhrkamp, 1976).
4. Cf. Rainer W. Trapp, *Analytische Ontologie* [*Analytic Ontology*] (Frankfurt am Main: Klostermann, 1976), 195ff.
5. As, earlier, did Jürgen Mittelstraß, 'Predication and the Return of the Same', in *Die Möglichkeit von Wissenschaft* [*The Possibility of Science*] (Frankfurt am Main: Suhrkamp, 1974), 145ff.
6. This expression stems from Edmund Husserl's *Erfahrung und Urteil*, ed. Ludwig Landgrebe (Hamburg: Meiner Verlag, 1972), 23ff. [trans. James S. Churchill and Karl Ameriks, *Experience and Judgment* (Evanston, IL: Northwestern University Press, 1973), §7 [= §6 – tr.], 27–8].
7. [The Erlangen school, or Erlangen constructivism, is founded on a philosophical anthropology deriving from Heidegger (see Wilhelm Kamlah, *Philosophische Anthropologie: Sprachkritische Grundlegung und Ethik*, 2nd edn [Mannheim: Bibliographisches Institut, 1973]) and mathematical logic (see Paul Lorenzen, *Lehrbuch der konstruktiven Wissenschaftstheorie*, 2nd edn

[Stuttgart: Metzler, 2000]). For recent discussions, see Peter Janich, *Das Maß der Dinge: Protophysik von Raum, Zeit und Materie* (Frankfurt am Main: Suhrkamp, 1997), and Jürgen Mittelstraß, *Der Konstruktivismus in der Philosophie im Ausgang von Wilhelm Kamlah und Paul Lorenzen* (Paderborn: Mentis, 2008).]
8. Nelson Goodman, *Fact, Fiction and Forecast*, 4th edn (Cambridge, MA: Harvard University Press, 1983), 61–2. Similarly, Nicholas Rescher, *Induction* (Oxford: Blackwell, 1980), ch. 10. It applies for both thinkers that metaphysics is inhibited by the exclusivity of methodological selection.
9. See *Metaphysics* 982b: 'if it was to escape ignorance that men studied philosophy, it is obvious that they pursued science for the sake of knowledge, and not for any practical utility'.
10. Gisbert Hasenjaeger, *Einführung in die Grundbegriffe und Probleme der modernen Logik* [*Introduction to the Fundamental Concepts and Problems of Modern Logic*] (Freiburg and Munich: Alber, 1962), 31.
11. W. V. O. Quine, *Methods of Logic* (Cambridge, MA: Harvard University Press, 1982), 210.
12. See the subtitle of his major work, *Individuals: An Essay in Descriptive Metaphysics* (London: Methuen, 1959).
13. W. V. O. Quine, *Ontological Relativity and Other Essays* (New York: Columbia University Press, 1969), 68.
14. One can schematise the two questions in this way:

1. What is that?—: a,? sought: F
2. What does that mean?—: F,? sought: a.

It is noteworthy that an F for a cannot be sought, if a is not already characterised through a G; that just as well a for an F cannot be sought, if nobody already has Fb. – Moreover the question 'What does that mean?' is interpretable not only semantically but also explanatorily. In this sense I ask myself, 'What does that mean?' when something that is the case happens or occurs to me that I 'can't figure out', that I cannot explain to myself. In this reading, the question, 'What does that mean?', is a counterpart to the question, 'What is that?', only in that this is not about the questionable classification of an *individual*, but rather the questionable explanation of an *event*, that is perhaps interpreted as a sign of something concealed (something in the past or in the future).

1. What does that mean?—: p, ? sought: $q \rightarrow p$.

15. Cf. Aristotle, *Topics*, 103b20.
16. W. V. O. Quine, 'Two Dogmas of Empiricism', in *From a Logical Point of View* (Cambridge, MA: Harvard University Press, 1953), 22.
17. [Goethe, *Faust*, trans. Walter Arndt, 2nd edn (New York: Norton, 2001), First Part, 382–3.]
18. Cf. Konrad Lorenz, *Behind the Mirror: A Search for the Natural History of Human Knowledge* (New York: Harcourt Brace Jovanovich, 1977).
19. Cf. Schelling: 'The *I* think, *I* am is, since Descartes, the fundamental error of all knowledge; the thinking is not my thinking, nor the being my being, for everything is only God, or the All.' *Aphorismen zur Einleitung in die Naturphilosophie* [*Aphoristic Introduction to Nature-Philosophy*, hereafter *Aphorisms*, SW I/7, 148]. In principle, Schelling simply sacrifices the generalisation of existence from the 'I think'.

20. Kant, *Critique of Pure Reason*, B 793, A 765.
21. Schelling, *Einleitung zu dem Entwurf eines Systems der Naturphilosophie* §4 [SW I/3, 279, trans. Keith R. Peterson as *Introduction to the Outline of a System of the Philosophy of Nature*, in *First Outline*, 198].
22. Cf. Bernulf Kanitscheider, 'On Schelling's "Speculative Physics" and Some Elements of an Idealistic Epistemology in Contemporary Cosmology', in Reinhard Heckmann, Hermann Krings and Rudolf W. Meyer (eds), *Natur und Subjektivität: Zur Auseinandersetzung mit der Naturphilosophie des jungen Schellings* [*Nature and Subjectivity: An Analysis of the Nature-Philosophy of the Young Schelling*] (Stuttgart-Bad Canstatt: Frommann-Holzboog, 1985), 239–64, here 239ff.
23. 'Satz und Tatsache' ['Proposition and Fact'], in Günther Patzig, *Sprache und Logik* (Göttingen: Vandenhoek and Ruprecht, 1970), 73.
24. Patzig, *Sprache und Logik*, 74.
25. Hasenjaeger, *Einführung*, 155. [Hogrebe refers here to Andrzej Mostowski, 'Über den Begriff einer Endlichen Menge', *Comptes rendus des séances de la Société des Sciences et des Lettres de Varsovie*, Classe III, vol. 31 (1938), S. 13–20 – tr.]
26. Cf. George S. Boolos and Richard C. Jeffrey, *Computability and Logic* (Cambridge: Cambridge University Press, 1974), 147.
27. A572/B600ff.
28. Of course, this does not affect the fact that in infinite domains, it often cannot be decided if Fx or $\bar{F}x$. For discourses which replace 'true' with 'provable', such as for example in intuitionist logic, the *tertium non datur* [law of excluded middle] is therefore not universally valid.
29. *CPR* A573/B601. This is from Chapter Three, Section Two, 'The Transcendental Ideal (*Prototypon transcendentale*)'.
30. Hasenjaeger, *Einführung*, 35.
31. Ibid., 35. For this reason Hasenjaeger replaces the Catalogue C_1 with an improved Catalogue C_2, which is for all of the cases in C_1 where the applicability of a quality for a is not specified, the non-applicability of this quality for *a* is noted, etc.
32. So far as I see it, this procedure of Kant has not yet been understood in this way. This is the passage to interpret: 'we nevertheless find on closer investigation that this idea, as an original concept, excludes a multiplicity of predicates, which, as derived through others, are already given, or cannot coexist with one another; and that it refines itself to a concept thoroughly determined a priori, and thereby becomes the concept of an individual object that is thoroughly determined merely through the idea, and then must be called an ideal of pure reason' (*CPR* A573–4/B601–2). Peter Rohs, whom we can thank for what is probably the clearest study of the matter (*Kants Prinzip der durchgängigen Bestimmung alles Seienden*, *Kant-Studien* 69 (1978), 170–80), also does not sort this passage out (cf. 174).
33. *CPR* A576/B604.
34. *CPR* A575–6/B603–4.
35. *CPR* A576/B604.
36. *CPR* A578/B606.
37. Cf. *CPR* A578–9/B606–7.
38. *CPR* A579/B607.
39. *CPR* A574/B602.

40. Tugendhat's formal semantics cannot explain this phenomenon.
41. Aristotle, *De Interpretatione* 19b.
42. [In English in the original.]
43. [In English in the original.]
44. *Philosophy of Mythology* [SW II/1, 283].
45. [SW II/1, 287.]
46. [SW II/1, 287–8.]
47. [SW II/1, 288.]
48. *CPR* A578/B606.
49. Schelling [SW II/1, 287].
50. Cf. §7 above.
51. On this, see Erhard Oeser's instructive work *Die antike Dialektik in der Spätphilosophie Schellings* [*The Ancient Dialectic in Schelling's Late Philosophy*] (Vienna and Munich: Oldenbourg, 1965), esp. Part 2, entitled 'Die Potenzlehre als Verknüpfung von Kant und Aristoteles', 66ff.
52. *Philosophy of Mythology* [SW II/1, 288]. Cf. the following.
53. [SW II/1, 288.]
54. [Schelling here refers to Aristotle's στέρησις [*Beraubung*, privation], see, e.g., *Metaphysics* 10004b27.]
55. *Philosophy of Mythology* [SW II/1, 289]. Cf. the following.
56. *Philosophy of Mythology* [SW II/1, 290].
57. *Philosophy of Mythology* [SW II/1, 290].
58. *Philosophy of Mythology* [SW II/1, 290].
59. *Philosophy of Mythology* [SW II/1, 293].
60. *Philosophy of Mythology* [SW II/1, 291].
61. [*TLP* 3.11.]
62. Here I conjugate Russell with Munitz. Cf. M. Munitz, *Cosmic Understanding* (Princeton, NJ: Princeton University Press, 1986), ch. 6, 'The Boundless', especially pp. 228f. [Italicised phrase above in English in the original – tr.]
63. [This is Hogrebe's insertion.]
64. *Philosophy of Mythology* [SW II/1, 285].
65. *Philosophy of Mythology* [SW II/1, 292].
66. *Philosophy of Mythology* [SW II/1, 292].
67. *Philosophy of Mythology* [SW II/1, 292].
68. [SW II/1, 294. *Das Nichtseyende*, non-being, refers to μὴ ὄν above.]
69. [SW II/1, 575ff. See esp. SW II/1, 585f.]
70. [SW II/1, 293.]

IV.

Predication and Genesis:
The Ages of the World

> The past is known, the present is discerned, the future is intimated. The known is narrated, the discerned is presented, the intimated is prophesied.[1]

With these propositions etched into stone, Schelling begins the introduction to *The Ages of the World*. They promise the reader knowledge, discernment and intimation. Taken together, the narrated, the presented and the prophesied are to be 'the development of a living, actual being'[2] or a biography. Not a biography of some arbitrary being, but of a 'primordially living' one, thus a biography 'of the oldest of beings'. The only question is: what evidence do we have available for this biography, from where do we gain information concerning something supposed to be oldest? Here Schelling introduces a principle that has behind it the representation of an auto-epistemic universe and can be formulated as *the proposition concerning the conservation of knowledge of beginnings* [*Anfangswissenserhaltungssatz*]. Since the energies that have produced the universe have produced it such that *ab initio* it is also active epistemically, what is first in knowledge is propagated in all its productions. Schelling puts it thus: 'Created out of the source of things and the same as it, the human soul is conscientious of creation [*hat eine… Mitwissenschaft der Schöpfung*].'[3] *Mitwissenschaft* means the Latin *conscientia*, an expression that, in philosophical terminology, designates consciousness. If consciousness is in fact to be understood by *Mitwissenschaft*, we are essentially witnesses, or in Greek, 'martyrs', martyrs, according to Schelling, to the beginning.

This beginning refers to the first, which is first in view of all development. Development and the beginning of development is always something physical that is older still than the physical universe; what is first, therefore, and 'from which everything begins, even the development of divine life'.[4] The theory of this first in all development is not the physics of the universe, but rather precedes it; it is metaphysics or, more precisely, protophysics. Its material is that from which a God, a world and a human being have emerged. The turbulent process of this emergence is the objective of *The Ages of the World*.

We have therefore abandoned Schelling's metaphorical language of beginnings since it demands the introduction of a certain sway into the thought-rhythms of *The Ages of the World*. We must equally endeavour not to let ourselves be anaesthetised by the toxic effect of his hazy metaphorics. So that this does not occur, I would immediately like to break up the continuous, organic discourse of Book I of *The Ages of the World* in order to establish the reconstructive cornerstones of our discussion. We will begin with the foundations of *The Ages of the World*'s argument, which Schelling himself introduced as a piece of predication theory. By this means we will reach a first antithesis, between pronominal and predicative being, which Schelling here understands as the antithesis of an original negation and an original affirmation. The attempt to resolve this antithesis by way of propositional being leads to what in my view is one of the central lessons of the first book of *The Ages of the World*, the theory of predicative rotation: propositional being falls back into the antithesis of pronominal versus predicative being, is rebuilt, collapses again and so forth. Schelling takes the brain-twisting event of an exploding and imploding propositional structure as a proto-ontic energy source, as a wheel turning eternally in itself. We are here dealing with a construction wanting to grasp the energy of becoming that grounds all the products of becoming up to the present, and remains disastrous for every proposition. This dimension is, according to Schelling's theory, the insuperably irrational presupposition of the sphere of reason, the turbulent chaos in the depths of all order.

That there is any exit at all from this dimension is quite a difficult problem even for Schelling. Its solution consists in nothing less than explaining the realisation of stable identity relations, the emergence of space and time or, in short, the emergence of the universe, that is, the emergence of true propositions. But this minor detail will no longer irritate whoever has accompanied us thus far.

§ 14 The predication-theoretical venture of *The Ages of the World*

Schelling does not defend the more common *theory of inherence* (of predicates inhering in substance), but an *identity theory of predication*: what holds of the subject term is precisely what holds of the predicate term:

$$Fa \rightarrow (\exists x)(x = a \wedge Fx), \text{ or also: } (x)[(Fx \rightarrow (\exists y)(Gy \wedge x = y)]$$

In Schelling's words, 'The true meaning of every judgment, for instance, A is B, can only be this: *that which* is A is *that which* is B, or *that which* is A and *that which* is B, are one and the same.'[5] It is unmistakable that Schelling here defends a construal of 'judgment' characteristic of predicate calculus. This becomes more definite in what follows:

> Therefore a doubling already lies at the bottom of the simple concept: A in this judgment is not A, but 'something = x that A is'. Likewise, B is not B, but 'something = x, that B is,' and not this (not A and B for themselves) but the 'x that is A' and 'the x that is B' is one and the same, that is, the same x.[6]

From this it follows, in Schelling's sense, that every element of the judgement *Fa*, as *a* and as *F*, already has in itself the structure of judgement. For *a* is an *x* and *F* is an *x*, so that *Fa* is a judgement of judgements. From the fact that *a x* and *F x* is, the third judgement *follows*, as the judgement of judgements, having an inferential character:

1. $a = x$
2. *Fx*
3. *Fa*

For Schelling, the triple structure of the judgement *Fa* arises 'of itself' from his characterisation of the judgement in terms of predicate calculus. He puts this consequence thus:

> the copula [*Band*] in the judgment is what is essential and that which lies at the bottom of all the parts. The subject and the predicate are each for themselves already a unity and what one by and large calls the copula just indicates the unity of these unities. Furthermore, the judgment is then already exemplified in the simple concept and the conclusion is already contained in the judgment. Hence, the concept is just the furled judgment and the conclsion is the unfurled judgment.[7]

Schelling avers that this explanation of the judgement is no marginal phenomenon either in itself, that is, on logical grounds alone, or for *The Ages of the World*'s real argumentation, but rather has an essential significance in what immediately follows. This argumentation is concerned, according to his comment, with

> remarks written here for a future and most highly desirable treatment of the noble art of reason [= logic, W.H.] because the knowledge of the general laws of judgment must always accompany the highest science. But one does not philosophize for novices or for those ignorant of this art. Rather, they are to be sent away to school...[8]

Thus Schelling leaves no clarity wanting: *without* a knowledge of logic, *The Ages of the World* will also remain incomprehensible, although naturally it does not become comprehensible with this knowledge *alone*. It is here important only that Schelling gives a clear disavowal that logic in speculation thinks it is able to dispense with all obscurantism. Materially considered, these methodological reflections accompany, in the introductory parts of the first book, the introduction of the antithesis of pronominal and predicative being that we have already become familiar with in Schelling's last lectures from the years 1847 and 1850 in the Berlin Academy of Sciences.[9]

This elementary lesson of *The Ages of the World* is present in all of the surviving fragments, both in Draft I (1811) and in Draft II (1813). So is the reconnection of this lesson to the development of the theory of judgement taken above from Draft III (1815).[10] In this respect Schelling's wrestling with *The Ages of the World* was therefore never deposed, remaining his philosophy until his death. Among the fragments is found exactly such a sentence as binds the systematic outline of the three planned books of *The Ages of the World* to the theory of predication, according to which every predication, as we have seen according to Schelling's statement of it, already contains in itself the theory of the concept, of judgement and of inference. Accordingly, the three books of *The Ages of the World* are conceived *moreover* as corresponding to the macrostructure of the project in general:

> For if the past stands before us only in the concept and in science, but the present is a matter of subsumption and of judgment, for which apart from the universal concept, another concept, still not enough to satisfy the breadth and depth of knowledge, is required, then by contrast there remains…[11]

The fragment breaks off here, but it is not hard to guess that in the third part the future will be brought into connection with inference. The fragmentary subordinate clause may perhaps be completed thus: then by contrast the future is to vindicate the inference. The entire concept of *The Ages of the World* therefore implies the resources of traditional logic, the theory of the concept, judgement and inference as the principle of its internal structure. And if there were otherwise no further warrant for our approach to the first book of *The Ages of the World*, this evidence alone already attests to the legitimacy of the attempt to tackle, using the theory of predication as a guide, the interpretation of *The Ages of the World* as a piece of speculation that is verified in itself and therefore verifiable.

§ 15 Original negation and original affirmation

In initio erat aliquid [In the beginning was Something whatever]. Before the world was, Something whatever already was. In the pre-worldly fog of not-knowing, we only have this: the absolute undetermined object of our referentiality. Pursuant to its indetermination, this object is still indifferent regarding its qualification as something to which singular termini or predicates refer. It is not specifiable and not characterisable. It is what it is, and only that.

And only that? What is it if it is what it is? With this question, the beginning indetermination, the diffuse indifference, breaks out immediately. As soon as we ask what Something whatever is, the question has already established two things: that Something whatever is Something whatever. We already have Something whatever that was Something whatever before there was a world. This means that the original fiction of an absolutely undetermined and therefore diffusely unitary Something whatever has immediately disintegrated into a duplicity: into one Something whatever, that we named *pronominal* being, and that Schelling elsewhere[12] names *quoddative being*, and into another Something whatever that we named *predicative being*, and that Schelling elsewhere correspondingly names *quiddative being*. We can readily concede that the original diffuse and unitary *aliquid* [Something whatever] is initially only available in this opposition, although we naturally remain oriented towards the original diffuse unity of the *aliquid*, because otherwise we would have nothing at all.

What is so cumbersomely expressed is certainly easier to get with Schelling's identity theory of predication, and he also introduces it here. According to it, the original unitary *aliquid* is simply that x for which both a and F can hold and which we can only have as a and F or finally as Fa. Schelling expresses this in this way: 'The true meaning of this unity that has been asserted in the beginning is therefore this: "one and the same = x"' is as much the unity as it is the antithesis.'[13]

Schelling immediately grasps that, indeed, as we have seen, we can only grasp the original and diffuse unitary *aliquid* through the form of a particular something as the Something whatever, that is, as the antithesis of pronominal and predicative being. He interprets this antithesis to mean that what is called pronominal being is not what is called predicative being. This is to say: the quality that Something whatever has at first as an individual, and indeed has *only* as such, must be distinguished from the quality that it has insofar as it has predicates. Something whatever as an individual is at first mere self, blank positivity, a matter [*Sachheit*] without qualities. That is, the characterisation of Something whatever purely as an individual is at first simply the negation of any predicative determinations. In this respect, Schelling also calls pronominal being *original negation*. Considered purely for itself, it opposes predicative being, and is simply for others, pure characterisability without conveyance, and in this respect, blank negativity. Schelling calls this *original affirmation*. Certainly, both moments are just as dependent on each other as they remain to be distinguished from each other. In the last judgement it is in this distinguishability that they enter into a final engagement. Whatever we are looking for before the world, that beginning *aliquid*, must be approached in this final engagement as what has become First. For 'both of the opposed potencies, the eternally negating potency and the eternally affirming potency, and the unity of both, make up the one, inseparable, primordial being [*Urwesen*]'.[14] Schelling illustrates the foundational duplicity of original negation and original affirmation, within which we can immediately grasp the diffuse *aliquid*, with multifarious variations.[15] For him, the pronominal being is 'ipseity [*Seinheit*]', 'being its own [*Eigenheit*]' and 'dislocation [*Absonderung*]'. Predicative being is 'love' as 'the nothing of being its own'. It is the 'being of all beings', 'baseless for itself' and 'conveyed by nothing'. The pronominal being must first 'make ground' as the 'eternal force of ipseity, of egoity'. Predicative being is 'the outwardly surging, expanding, self-presenting being'. Overall, the 'being [*Wesen*]', the pronominal 'eternal force of ipseity, of retreating back into itself, of in-itself-being', is before all 'force'.

It is important for Schelling that we recognise not only this antithesis as such, but especially the 'originality of the opposition'. It is important that they therefore cannot be derived apart from each other or reduced to one of the two. He admits that humans probably have a 'natural predilection for the affirmative just as much as they turn away from the negative': 'Most people would find nothing more natural than if everything in the world were to consist of pure gentleness and goodness, at which point they would soon become aware of the opposite.'[16]

In ancient myths, where our consciousness [*Mitwissenschaft*] of the beginning could express itself in an even more undisguised manner, this opposition turns up as the opposition between light and darkness, and between the masculine and the feminine. But in later times, 'ages more and more alienated from that primordial feeling', attempts were often made to nullify reductively this antithesis, primarily by seeking to remove the negative force that excludes everything predicative. Hence one attempted 'to resolve fully the incomprehensible in comprehension or (like Leibniz) in representation [*Vorstellung*]'.[17] Moreover: 'Idealism, which really consists in the denial and non-acknowledgment of that negating primordial force, is the universal system of our times.'[18]

Schelling will retain this position regarding idealism up to his late philosophy. He will conceive idealism as a theory of predicative being, which either has the non-conceptual positivity of being external to itself or presupposes it, as *negative philosophy*. This first obtains, through a theory of pronominal being as *positive philosophy*, as a necessary correction, supplement and consummation. Furthermore, from the perspective excerpted here, it becomes clear why Schelling in his late philosophy after *The Ages of the World* was developing a *philosophy of mythology*. As we have already heard, *mythos* is essentially closer to the primordial feeling of that antithesis than later times. For this reason, it cannot be an absurd enterprise to make the *mythos* transparent with regard to such findings in order to render eloquent the traces of an ancient knowledge of that primordial being. Schelling first tackled an enterprise with this objective with his small tract, *On the Deities of Samothrace* (1815), published as an addendum to *The Ages of the World*. (There is therefore nothing in the so-called late philosophy that Schelling has not already devised within the radius of *The Ages of the World*.) Even in *The Ages of the World* itself, he refers to the mythic in order to authenticate the ancient knowledge of said opposition of negating force and affirming force. They are

> the same as the two primordial beings in the Persian teaching, one being a power insisting on closure and the darkening of the being and the other insisting on its outstretching and revelation. Both do not conduct themselves as one, but as two Godheads.[19]

In order not to give the impression here that his theory is about an original dualism rather than an original *duplicity of the same*, Schelling immediately adds:

> But it still remains that 'one and the same = x' is both principles (A and B). But not just in accordance with the concept, but really and actually. Hence 'the same = x' that is the two unities must again be the unity of both unities and with the intensified antithesis is found the intensified unity.[20]

We already know that this intensified unity is the engagement in formal propositions in which pronominal being and predicative being engage through propositional being. But we have not gone that far yet.

Certainly, the crucial question is how that antithesis and contradiction of original negation and original affirmation happens at all. Why could the original diffuse unity, the absolutely indifferent Something whatever, not remain attached to its blessed indifference, in which there are verily no edges and borders, where there are no distinctions, yet it is everything? Schelling does not evade this question:

> A transition from unity to contradiction is incomprehensible. For how should what is in itself one, whole and perfect, be tempted, charmed, and enticed to emerge out of this peace? The transition from contradiction to unity, on the other hand, is natural…[21]

This means: the departure from the originally indifferent unity is inconceivable in the sense that it cannot be motivated, while it is valid for the restoration of a unity that has been lost to antitheses.

What cannot be motivated, and yet happens, occurs blindly. But why? The diffuse homogeneity of the in itself indifferent *aliquid* has everything in itself and nothing; it exists, and it does not exist; there are still here no contradictions of any kind *as such*; and hence there are contradictions with a contradicting force: the original *aliquid* simply has a non-declarative being. Hence a simple *sub-identic* homogeneity suits it. It is x and, as such, it is simultaneously $x = x$ and $x \neq x$. It is the case that that which has everything is simultaneously that which is lacking in everything. This is an explosive mixture that is sensitive to a decisive event since in itself it cannot mean anything. The disintegration of the homogeneity of the first diffuse Something whatever, the primordial explosion, is therefore something that 'can happen rather only when a violent power blindly breaks the unity in the jostling between the necessity and the impossibility to be'.[22] This is certainly not an explanation, but at least it is a speculative comment on the question asked. An answer in the precise sense of an explanation is not possible, because for this we would have to appeal to assumptions of principle and fulfilled boundary conditions, about which nothing can be said in this pre-worldly fog of not-knowing.

But if the primordial explosion happened once, the blind energy will be released immediately, on the one side to be energy and on the other side to be determinate, and in the end taken together, for energy to be something determinate. All three energies repel each other in their obstinate self-attachment [*Eigensinn*], and act towards each other as if the other does not exist. *Something whatever*, namely x, exclusively wants to be: *(∃x) (. . . x . . .)*; *what* can be, namely *F*, exclusively wants to be some kind of *F*, and hence to be *Φ*; *that* something can be something, namely in the end *Fa*, exclusively wants that *Φx*. This metaphoric formulation factually makes sense in that in the condition that something exists, it is *not* initially said that there are predicates, but rather something to which they accord; that this condition does *not* likewise say that existence is a quality to which predicates accord but rather the quality of predicates means that they are not empty; and that this condition likewise and finally does *not* say that predicates and things alone suffice, but rather that there must be a proposition: *(∃x) (Fx ∧ x = a)*; and that fourthly and finally – as we will see later – propositions are also not sufficient, which indeed guarantees the criterial sense of being for us but not the definitory: Existence is the definitory quality of the universe.

Schelling expresses it like this:

> If the unity [this means: propositional being] is that which has being, then the antithesis, that is, each of the opposites [means: pronominal being and predicative being], can only be that which does not have being. And, in turn, if one of the opposites, and thereby the antithesis [this means: of pronominal being and predicative being], has being, then the unity [this means: propositional being] can only retreat into that which does not have being.[23]

Since each moment now 'has the same claim to be that which has being',[24] we require a formula of compatibility. This must take measure that, in this syndrome of claims to be, it is only a matter of making a start and therefore must throw out a formula for the beginning that integrated the conflicting energies. We universally require for beginnings a *start potential*, a *continuation potential* and a *structure potential*. Schelling grasps this potential with the expression 'potencies', whereby it is first of all advisable to trace this Latin expression back to the Greek δύναμις, despite Schelling's established allusion to the mathematical sense of power calculation. This here deals with a theory of beginning potentials or *protodynamics*.

To ameliorate the difficulties of an introduction to this theory, it is best that we proceed with a concrete example of a beginning: drawing a line. The set-up is the start potential, for example, chalk on a blackboard. In fact, there is such a point, but certainly not the realised chalk splotch, but rather the geometric point, so to speak, 'stigmatised' through it. In this example, it represents the sought-for beginning potential and its quality, which we take for its general characterisation, for each beginning is a *terminus a quo*. What is essential here is that the point is without extension in the geometric sense. The start potential generally lies in something that opposes it, but whose beginning, by acting negatively, it renders possible. Schelling also makes this clear with the same example: 'The beginning of the line is the geometrical point, but not because it extended itself but rather because it is the negation of all extension.'[25]

The beginning of the line is not the line. At the beginning lies that the line should be, but it is not yet; it is only wished for. What is wished for in the beginning is not yet, but then it is, and the beginning as such has passed, disappearing into the underworld, so to speak. One can also make these complicated relationships clear with the example of movement. Before the start of a race, for example, the runners pull themselves together. This is the negation of movement as such, although with this contraction of the musculature they are ready. The runners being fast out of the starting blocks is an overcoming of the beginning negation of movement. Or, to speak with Schelling:

> No beginning point (*terminus a quo*) of a movement is an empty, inactive point of departure. Rather it is a negation of the starting point and the actually emerging movement is an overcoming of this negation. If the movement was not negated, then it could not have been expressly posited. Negation is therefore the necessary precedent (*prius*) of every movement.[26]

We have to project on to the relationships of existential beginnings the peculiarity of the start potential, that is, the start contraction, which provides a beginning as initial potential, indeed, as the negation of what it is the beginning of. The beginning of existence is afterwards the negation of *what* begins to exist. Something whatever begins to be by being what it will not be: 'the beginning really only lies in the negation'.[27] And: 'negation is the first transition whatsoever from nothing into something'.[28]

As difficult as the relationships are here, the intuition is simply that the beginning potential lets *Something whatever* be in opposition to *what* can be. This characteristic is simply the more detailed determination of pronominal being as beginning being, as pure being for itself, as eternal No. The more graspable sense of this eternal No is that the beginning potential is straightaway an absolute singularity, namely Something whatever. It excludes anything that it encounters that would associate with it and nothing predicative is graspable yet. The absolutely individual eludes or negates all predicative determinations. That is why it is what has come before everything expressible: the individual is ineffable.

But it is just as clear that in this maximisation of the gravity of the singular, being with regard to itself, the whole domain of the predicative immediately emerges as something independent from it and becomes visible. However, the predicative remains dependent on a beginning being made in which the individual is available and upon which the predicative can find a mainstay on its own. This turns out to be, as Schelling so beautifully says:

> [What] laboriously proves itself and reveals itself as having being, has its ground in the negating potency. If there were not the No, then the Yes would be without force. No 'I' without the 'not-I' and in as much as the 'not-I' is before the 'I'.[29]

Here the 'I', the Yes, that which has being, stands for predicative being, the expressible, what requires what it is expressly about, just as the meaning of a predicate only gains support when there is something to which it is assigned or denied. Indeed, predicates are self-sustaining in relationship to individuals; they cannot be explained from this purely as individuals, but they are 'unsaturated' for themselves and require them as instances.

Related to the beginning, our *protodynamics* refers to the *continuation potential* of predicative being, which without the predicative Yes would immediately die away. Or more precisely, it would not lead to the beginning of something, but it would remain a simple flash of being. Predicative being as the continuation potential of the beginning is the condition in which Something whatever can be something manifest. It is hence the condition in which being becomes manifest and clear. This presupposes that pronominal being is predicatively subordinate in the sense that it is 'veiled' purely as predicative of the individual, in so far as purely as an individual, it negates itself. In this reciprocal negation, they are hostile to each other, each ready to annihilate the other 'because it only requires an inversion, a turning out of what was concealed and a turning into what is manifest, in order to transpose and, so to speak, transform, the one into the other'.[30]

This antagonism between the start potential and the continuation potential of the beginning as such cannot be taken away, and in the *protodynamics* can only be satisfied in such a way that it receives a covenant, so that the antagonism is made compatible in itself by a structure potential of the beginning.

It does not suffice for the beginning that Something whatever is and that it continues as Something whatever. Rather, it must also be ensured that it remains fixed and finds a form as anything that is Something whatever. This structure potential of the beginning is therefore indifferent towards the start and the continuation. This is the case when pronominal being and predicative being enter into an association that propositional being provides, which ensures *that Fa*, *that* Something whatever, has some kind of qualities. A dissipative compatibility structure builds itself over the antagonism between pronominal being and predicative being as a third potency.

> Just as the originary negation is the eternal beginning, this third is the eternal end. There is an inexorable progression, a necessary concatenation, from the first potency to the third. When the first potency is posited, the second is also necessarily posited, and both of these produce the third with the same necessity. Thereby the goal is achieved. There is nothing higher to be produced in this course.[31]

One could think that we have now come to the end of our beginning. We have in our stylised protodynamics made the antagonism of the original energies of the start potential and the continuation potential compatible with each other in a structure potential, and so it engenders something like a proto-state-of-affairs that makes

Something whatever compatible with its predicative determination. The singular and the predicative enter into a unity, that is, into a structure that admits of judgement. We would have therefore brought order to this relationship. But how stable is it? We must not forget that in our *protodynamics* we inherently only have to deal with the energy *potentials* of the beginning, not with something that actually exists. It turns out that our beautiful order is simply an internal order of possibilities, which are built with some necessity upon its qualities, but which remains an order of possibilities, each of which still has the same claim for itself as before to be the thoroughgoing actuality. The order we have achieved is impotent against this claim. The order loses its ordering force against it. What if the individual were thoroughly what has being? Or what if what has being were the predicative, or the propositional?

Each for itself can announce this claim and our predicative structure again falls apart:

> Yet having arrived at its peak, the movement of itself retreats back into its beginning; for each of the three has an equal right to be that which has being. The former differentiation and the subordination that followed from it is only a differentiation of the being, it is not able to sublimate the equivalence with regard to that which is as what has being. In a nutshell, it is not able to sublimate the existential parity.[32]

This collapse of the predicative structure is difficult to understand. Only when we respect that no structure of the beginning can bring to a standstill the dynamic of the becoming of being, its ontogenesis, does it make sense. It is not allowed, or otherwise we would postulate a resting being in the style of the Eleatics and then wonder why we have problems with movement.

Schelling himself declares that the collapse of the predicative structure as the final stroke of *protodynamics* is motivated by the need to take into account the phenomenality of becoming. Whoever in one fell swoop finished this predicative structure, and this means 'covered it over' by an immediately rigid superstructure, would also have brought the world process to a standstill in it. 'But if one begins thereby to posit as actually subordinated that which ought to be subordinated, what then does one have? One is already finished in the beginning. Everything has happened and there is no further progression.'[33]

Whoever therefore wants to include the possibility of becoming in the *protodynamics* will have to take into account a constant construction and repeated disintegration of the predicative structure. Or more precisely: this structure has not yet reached a stability that would remove it from its realisation. Put otherwise: its existence or non-existence is likewise contingent upon the destiny of the drive of being, just like the truth values of the principles of observation regarding the weather. What we have achieved structurally, therefore, cannot yet be separated from the situational.

§ 16 Predicative rotation

What we have reached are possible beginnings that never coincide with actual beginnings. How are we to understand this? Let us return to our geometrical image of the beginning, the line. Is there not here an *actual* beginning, namely, that point from which the tracing of the line begins? In fact, it is an *actual* beginning provided we are prepared to begin with *any* point *whatever*. But to begin at *any* point *whatever* means to make a *possible* beginning. The *determinate* point, that is, one 'chosen' by the nib of the pen, is meaningless in itself, and only stands for *any point whatever*. What we have been considering thus far are merely *example beginnings*. We only have an *actual* beginning when we have obtained the fixed *initial variables*. It could be objected here that the fact that we are able to discuss example beginnings already implies a reference to initial variables. Moreover, have we not thus far analysed the process of beginning precisely in its *generality*, thus fundamentally, already the initial variables? I believe that this question is in fact to be answered in the affirmative. What we yet lack is an *explicit* characterisation of the foregoing analysis in terms of this perspective. But we have not yet got this far. At present we really only have example beginnings and must inquire in more detail as to what it means if we want to take the process of becoming into account.

Until now we have only analysed the process in which anything whatever becomes a such-and-such. The analysis suggested that something is thereby 'finished', its biography having come to an end. With this, we would have brought the worldly process to a standstill, nothing moving any longer, and becoming would remain to be grasped. If we want our analysis to unlock the genetic aspect, we will have to extrapolate the biography of Something whatever in order that the process may continue. But how should we do this?

We began with pronominal being, made its antithesis to predicative being clear, and 'reconciled' both through propositional being. We have no other potential energies at our disposal. How then can a continuation of this process take place if our energy source is exhausted? We have no other option here: *continuation must take place as repetition*. What was always anything whatever can only become another anything whatever. What other it becomes is again only another example of that which it already was. In this way our biography repeats, giving a new example beginning in its fashion. We may therefore account for becoming as a style of *iteration* of the process analysed thus far. And we could add here that no other possibility is available to us. This implies that the iteration model stands for an inevitability that something disruptive has. Schelling accounts for this aspect by conceiving the iterative structure of becoming as 'a kind of circle', as a 'constant annular drive', as 'unremitting wheel' or, with James (3:6), as ὁ τροχός τῆς γενέσεως [the wheel of genesis].[34] The iterative structure of becoming, the retreating of the beginning process to its beginnings, attests that here we are always and only dealing with example beginnings that always anew document possible beginnings but not an actual one: 'There is certainly a beginning of the potency in accordance with its inherent possibility, but this is not an actual beginning.'[35] Strictly speaking, in this iteration, 'the concept of the beginning, like that of the end, again sublimates itself in this circulation'.[36] With this construction, according to Schelling, we have 'the consummate concept of that first nature'. Thus, 'we can also explain this first blind life as one that can find neither its beginning nor its end. In this respect we can say that it is *without* (veritable) beginning and *without* (veritable) end.'[37]

This constantly turning process is the energetic pulse of the universe, its beating heart, whose beat is perceptible in all emergence and passing. Yet it is perceptible only because the relative stability of the transient simultaneously attests to the fact that spatiotemporal being first becomes possible when this constant turning can be 'retarded'. Hence the original constant turning is indigenous to the universe, while what is unearthly [*unheimlich*] to us is the *mystery of the world* in the deep well of the past from which we would wish to be spared. They are forces of

> that inner life that incessantly gives birth to itself and again consumes itself that the person must intimate, not without terror, as what is concealed in everything, even though it is now covered up and from the outside has adopted peaceful qualities.[38]

This rotation of beings indicates an original, cosmic inconsistency, an 'abyss of thought',[39] something inexpressible, 'an eternally insatiable obsession'.[40] In a manuscript from a revision of Draft I of *The Ages of the World*, Schelling describes our shock at learning of this original cosmic inconsistency in an extremely graphic manner:

> When lightning flashes, and storm and torrential rain threaten to throw heaven and earth into confusion, unleashing the elements to clamor and rage, or when the solid ground of the earth tremors and quakes; or, most horrifyingly, when terrible wrath is ignited in human communities, destroying trust and friendship; when atrocities and abominations break forth, and all ties dissolve; in such times as these a person will feel just how much the old condition is still alive. When this happens everything becomes uncanny, just as in the most horrific witching hour.[41]

The scene is unquestionably impressively set. However, to illustrate the experience of inconsistency, we need only make the elementary question, to which predication is an answer, sufficiently penetrable so that the preliminary decision that has already been encountered with the question breaks down and opens up a view to something that, prior to meaning, understanding and reason, is powerless. The elementary question to which predication is an answer is simply the question 'What is it?' or in French, which is clearer in this case, '*Qu'est-ce que c'est?*', what is it that it is? The scale of this question is 'restricted' by the imputation: 'what it always is, is exactly what it is', and the question only makes sense within these restrictions. If we wished to make the limits of the question's scope porous, we could formulate it thus: what it always is, is that which it *perhaps* is; or even more precisely: what it always is, is that which it is *not*. That is, we must also take account of things that, since they are F's, are therefore not $\neg F$'s: $(x)\,(Fx \to \bar{F}x)$, or its equivalent $\neg(\exists x)\,(Fx)$. These schemas are after all not already always false on logical grounds; they are true in the case that *Fx* is false. But since we precisely do not *unquestionably* know whether *x* is an *F*, the question as such does not exclude a universe so structured that, in connection with that universe, we could never obtain a true answer. That is, we can acquire a questionable perspective on a world for which there is no true answer. This world is inconsistent in the weak sense, that is, consistent for false answers, inconsistent for all true answers. Such a world is on logical grounds alone not immediately impossible, although epistemically maximally unproductive, since informatively true sentences concerning it could not be realised. It is not therefore ruled out on logical grounds alone that there is such a universe, but if it were ours, we would have no knowledge of the world.

Yet do we have any? Have we not precisely learned from our contemporary scientific theories that there is absolutely no true knowledge in the definitive sense? Are we not exactly epistemically impotent? And isn't this simply because the structure of the world is incompatible with an epistemic potency? Aren't our epistemic claims simply obtained under false pretences, because we act as if things are precisely what they are, when we ask 'What is it'? And if we have done this for the world, have we not then also done this for ourselves? Who are we? Who am I? Are we perhaps indeed those who we are; am I not he who I am? With such questions the world slips away from us, we slip away from ourselves, just as the man who grasped the *mystery of the world* in Hofmannsthal's poem slipped away from himself:

> The deep well knows it certainly;
> And leaning there a man would know,
> But rising up, would lose it so.
> Would wildly talk, and make a song.[42]

Before reconciling ourselves to this consequence, which seems to leave only the recommendation of epistemic nihilism remaining to us,[43] we must pull ourselves together and mobilise that strength of soul that Schelling, at the beginning of *The Ages of the World*, called for as necessary for the reader thinking with him:

> It is not given to everyone to know the end and it is given to few to see the primordial beginnings of life and it is given to even

fewer to think through the whole of things from beginning to end. Imitation, rather than the inner drive, leads to a research that confuses the senses as if by an inevitable fate. Hence, inner fortitude [*Seelenstarke*] is necessary in order to keep a firm hold of the interrelation of movement from beginning to end.[44]

The more profound meaning of our construction of a universe, which is clearly logically possible but only logically compatible with false propositions and incompatible with true ones, should really be that, with Schelling and within the framework of our reconstruction, we must represent the initial state of the universe as a rotary 'urge towards existence', that is, an 'alternating positing'.[45] Having shown up to this point how a beginning may be thought *as exemplified*, that is, by establishing a predicative structure of the type Fx, each of the elements of this structure nevertheless has equal right to be, if indeed becoming is to be accessible to us; this structure will be supposed to be Fx, just as in our formula for the structure of the world: $(x) (Fx \rightarrow \bar{F}x)$, and with x we are again at the beginning, seeking an F or a G that it can become. In this way, the predicative procedure is iterated by rotation and does not yet provide anything solid, wills something to become but does not know what, remaining a churning, blind becoming in which all fixed differences remain engulfed. We may even make this unwieldy energy amenable so that we have recourse to the creative energy of a questionable predication and draw up a protocol for the inner dialogue in which the attempt at predication, for example, is set down so: what then is this? Looks like an animal, but is not, it is … it is somewhat plantlike, no, not that, but certainly has some remarkable properties, ah, a machine, no, or yes, a monster? (In truth we are dealing with…).

On the whole we may say that the rotary energetic pulse of the universe is particularly evident on the epistemic level when we ask, doubt, reflect or seek. In short, the phases of epistemic uncertainty, which are at the same time creative phases. Certainly these are phases that we cannot bear for long; we want to be delivered from thoughts of problem solving, from sought-for answers, from a literally 'redemptive idea', but the energy of the originally alternating positing is operative even in this phase. This is the general meaning of predicative rotation as the energy of becoming in everything: 'Hence, this is the first pulse, the beginning of that alternating movement that goes through the entirety of visible nature, of the eternal contraction and the eternal re-expansion, of the universal ebb and flow.'[46]

If by setting up the structure of predication as an example beginning that, provided that it was followed through, would present a finished, settled world, what we now have is a constantly churning world of sheer becoming without permanent structure, a blind rotation 'compelled by need'[47] to be, a raging necessitation: 'Nature strives for itself and does not find itself (*quaerit se natura, non invenit*).'[48] If predicative structure gave us a preliminary answer, but no motivating question, we now have simply a harrowing question, but no answer. Thus, our problem now is how we can 'apply the brakes' to this racing wheel, how we can grip it by its spokes, how this chaos can acquire structure or, with Schelling, 'How or by virtue of what was the life redeemed from this annular drive and led into freedom?'[49]

§ 17 From chaos to order

The predicative rotation does not allow the Something whatever to become a such-and-such. We have not once rightly viewed Something whatever, but rather what is dissimilar to itself (*sui dissimile*): 'It admittedly wants itself as such, but precisely this is impossible in an *immediate* way; in the very wanting itself [*im Wollen selbst*] it already becomes other and distorts itself...'[50] Linguistically there is certainly not much of a display with a universe that is only populated by a constantly distorted Something whatever. In antiquity, this world was debated as a Heraclitean universe, in which everything is subjugated to constantly flowing change. Plato even once suggests that one 'would have to introduce another language' for such a universe, and right away constructed a word that in the lexicon of this language belongs to the Heraclitean universe: 'it would have to be something like "not onetime so" (οὐδ' οὕτως) [...] expressed entirely undetermined (ἄπειρον λεγόμενον)'.[51] Of course, this is the only entry. If we want to get out of this universe of predicative rotation and its incapacity for language, we have to take care that pronominal, predicative and propositional being attain relative stability.

I would here like to draw upon an image for clarification. We can project a standing image on a screen with a film projector if we turn off the motor. This corresponds to the Parmenidean universe of our settled, initial world. We can also let the motor transport the film with an excessive speed and project on to the screen an optical flash in which we could not recognise anything at all. This effect corresponds to the rotary world or Heraclitean universe. Staying with this image, our task is therefore to set the running speed of the motor to the proper time of the happening of the image in order to achieve a flawless projection of the image. In other words, we must therefore retrieve pronominal, predicative, and propositional being from their absurd alternation. In other words, it has to succeed at putting the brakes on pronominal being *as* pronominal being, predicative being *as* predicative being, and propositional being *as* propositional being.[52] Since this cannot be done from the outside, these beginning potentials must submit themselves, and *give up being themselves*, as they surrender wanting to be everything, which is whatever the other is, and driven by this will, keeps them from being themselves. So long as they are 'driven by nature in the same fashion to be that which has being', they must

> all strive to be in one and the same locus, namely, in the locus of that which has being and hence, so to speak, to be in a single point. A reciprocal inexistence [*Inexistenz*] is demanded because they are incompatible and when one has being, then the others must be without being. Hence this necessity can only terminate if all of the potencies have sacrificed, in the same fashion, being that which has being.[53]

This renunciation of the imperative to be is altogether a recognition that something other is what has being, a something other that has pronominal, predicative and propositional being. What can this be? It can no longer be an energy potential because we have that completely before us. It would therefore have to be, as Schelling says, 'a lack of potency in itself'.[54] It is therefore what makes place for and gives space to all of the beginning potentials. It is therefore something that is the placeholder of all example beginnings. It is not itself an example, but rather *that of which these examples are examples*.

It is obvious that this can only have the meaning of a beginning variable. This is a meaning that we had always *secretly* treated in our discussion of example beginnings. How can this beginning variable be more precisely characterised? It is for each beginning, each initiatory beginning, as well as for each ending, for the throbbing of becoming as well as what is abiding and immobile. As what endows beginnings with space it is what makes beginnings possible. What makes beginnings possible is also what we attach to the word 'freedom', which is here just the presupposition that, for example, with the pen we *can* begin the train of the line at *any* point *whatever*. Based on the realised beginning, the beginning variable is itself no beginning and is not something; but yet as the beginning dimension of all beginnings it is nonetheless somehow something. Since it is itself not involved in the happening of a beginning, the beginning dimension is not the beginning or ending of anything, that is, it is without time and place, it already is when something begins to be. Along with Schelling, one can call this beginning variable 'beyond that which has being [*das Überseyende*]' (τὸ ὑπερόν).[55] From a Platonic perspective, this is the idea of the good of which it is said, 'it is not what is being, but what exceeds being in age and power'.[56]

This all sounds somewhat dramatic and it is the extreme of what philosophy can do. But at this point we do not need to throw in the argumentative towel if we just keep tight to the explication of the sense of the variables. In relation to our starting problem: if we drill the predicative rotation down on a structurally compatible tempo, the result is simply the following. However exuberantly our construction of an absurd iteration of the predicative processes of the pronominal, predicative and propositional being in a rotary process of displacement was carried out, it will clear itself up if we just expressly insert it into the beginning variable. Because it is related to any predicative beginnings, the beginning variable is the predicative structure dimension for Φx. It gives all predications space and makes them explicit and assigns a structure to their elements: the position of the pronoun and the position of the predicate are set as these elements in order to be capable of being a proposition.

Since only propositional being in itself already provides the structure potential for pronominal and predicative being, it is what by its nature is most innately similar to the meaning of the variable, because the variable Φx makes space for *that Fx* or *that p*, and lets it be pronounced or is the utterance for *that p*. The beginning variable creates place for the condition, that *p*. As such it is the absolute condition, not itself a proposition but rather a pre-proposition, or absolute proposition, or propositional variable, or the dimension of a proposition, what Schelling also calls spirit (*Geist*). Through the natural proximity of propositional being to that in which it finds space there arises a symmetry break between the beginning potentials, and 'that equivalence (equipollence) automatically terminates'.[57] In order to be able to instantiate the predicative variable, propositional being must come forth and predicative and pronominal being must retreat, that is, its place *as* pronoun and *as* predicate *in toto* must take in propositional content. This is the origination of predicative space and predicative time.

> Therefore, in order to come into relationship with that which is beyond having being [*das Überseyende*] [this means: to engage in the predicative structure], eternal nature must take on that state within itself in which what is free in it [this means: propositional being] elevates itself above its Other and becomes the immediate subject [this means: the instance] of an in itself unfathomable spirit [this means: of the propositional variable]. But each of the other two principles [this means: pronominal and predicative being] establishes itself in its appropriate place in such a way that the first potency [= pronominal being] occupies the lowest place, the second [= predicative being] the middle place, and the third [= propositional being] the highest place.[58]

Schelling himself also characterised this structure fashioning process as that by which the world becomes capable of predication such that nature in this process becomes 'the merely expressible' in which it simultaneously renounces 'being what is expressive, being what has being [*Seyende zu Seyn*]'.[59] This means for us: it cedes this claim to the propositional variable, which becomes the ultimately expressive, the anonymous utterance, the first event (ὄν εἰμι). The whole beginning potential, pronominal being as the original negation, is thereby at once 'that force of the beginning posited in the expressible and exterior'; but it remains the inconsistent past of the consistent and as such the original seed of visible nature: 'Nature is an abyss of the past.'[60] This means: 'A Before and an After first emerge here, an actual articulation and thereby a soothing.'[61] Space and time emerge as the conditions of articulation of the propositional, of meaning. As such, space and time are simultaneously forms that repress the original rotary madness. 'The inexpressible becomes the expressible in relationship to what is for it the word.'[62] But the word is to it the pre-existing meaning of the variables because, as 'beyond that which has being [*das Überseyende*]', it 'cannot anywhere in itself be that which has being. It can do so only relationally with respect to an Other.'[63]

But whence that other, the expressive stuff of its instantiation? Schelling ponders various answers here, among them that the variable is precisely what is not Not-Variable, according to 'the ancient doctrine of the thesis from which the antithesis follows'.[64] But this trick 'could at best be a dialectical and never an historical, i.e., an authentically scientific'[65] answer. Schelling does not attempt such surprise attacks in order to avoid the threat of dualism. He could simply point out that the propositional variable, like any variable, innately has a pronominal character. This lets them be explained as the later fruit of pronominal being, out of which the stuff for its instantiation is obtained. The variable has 'gotten something over and done with, i.e., posited it as the past'.[66] This means: that other, the stuff of the instantiation of variables, is related to what is past to it. It hence has a 'life that circulates in a continuing circle as an eternal past in it'.[67] It broadly looks like a self-instantiation of the variables, and in a certain sense it is: the instances are solely from the *old* stuff of the variables; they are only from the 'blind' stuff of their past and from their past inconsistency and unconsciousness. With each instantiation it first becomes 'seeing' and it 'sees' what it already was. And this means: it becomes *conscious* by instantiation.

A structure is finally gained from the unconscious tumult of predicative iteration and beginning inconsistency. 'Something figural comes to be out of the non-figural.'[68] A universe that admits of predication and consistency originated. The model of this genesis is an inference from inconsistent premises, a *self*-discovery, the process of becoming conscious, the transition from 'Something whatever' to 'Somebody or other' [*irgendwer*]. Schelling understood this *pronominal difference* as result: only when Something whatever has found *itself* can Somebody or other speak. This is thoroughly equivocal. It *first* says that we can first speak about Something or other when Something or other 'stands firm' as (x) (x = x) and thereby has become something expressible. It *secondly* says that Something whatever has come to itself and thereby can be something expressive: 'what wants to articulate itself must first come to itself'.[69] But how can Something whatever come to itself? Schelling describes this according to the model of seeking and finding: 'everything that should come to itself must seek itself. There must therefore be something in it that seeks and something that is sought.'[70] One can also clarify this in this way: Something whatever in us seeks to be expressible and what it therefore seeks is Something whatever expressive through which it is expressed. According to Schelling, this *seeking after the speaker* is the yearning [*Sehnsucht*] of nature[71] to become expressible, that is, to liberate itself from blind predicative iteration to a structure that admits of predication; that is, to attain a structure of meaning to become capable of propositions, to escape madness [*Wahnsinn*] and to be 'manically peaceful [*wahn-friedlich*]'. That this yearning originates is simply the magical effect of the propositional dimension. The turmoil of becoming, the beginning inconsistency, the original nonsense, breaks with the magic of meaning.[72] This was just one and magically becomes everything.

Our biography of the most ancient being [*Wesen*] has thereby come to a preliminary conclusion. The pronominal difference between Something whatever and Somebody or other is established and because of this, consciousness and a universe has emerged from the structure that cannot admit predicative iteration. But 'the forces of that consuming fire still slumber in life, only pacified and, so to speak, exorcised by that *word* by which the one became the all'.[73]

§ 18 Self-organisation and unity

There is no question that Schelling causes the understanding enormous difficulties by setting up a fourth dimension, which does not of course settle the cut-throat competition in the three-dimensional possibility space but rather makes it structure-apt, after a fashion. This above all because the competition itself belongs to the past of that fourth instance, of which it is not independent, but is only that which the harnessing of wild relations makes possible: it passes away into this stabilisation, passes away into every structure, but constantly remains its threatening past, the latent 'no' to all structure.

Schelling's fourth instance resembles what Hermann Haken will quite vividly designate as 'the enslaving principle' in self-organising processes.[74] According to this, diffuse kinematic flows in an energy supply enter into a kinematic structure that by 'enslaving' competing kinematic patterns, itself arises through one of these patterns. Haken also calls the 'enslaving' pattern the 'regulator'. The latter is equally a selector among competitors, just as, finally, it is their speculative *dompteur* [trainer]. In all processes in open systems, such as, for example, in cloud formation, fluid processes and so on, the same drama is always repeated, namely, how 'individual parts are induced to arrange as if by an invisible hand, while on the other hand individual systems first create this invisible hand through their cooperation. We will call this invisible, all-ordering hand a "regulator".'[75] Precisely because this regulator is not something that enters into proceedings from outside, but belongs to the manner in which it self-organises, it is simply the regulative principle of self-organisation, which, with some purposiveness, 'transports' chaotic relations into organised states.

Now, since this 'guidedness of the emergence of order from chaos', as Haken emphasises, is 'thoroughly independent of the material substrate on which proceedings are played out', the conjecture suggests itself to him

> that purposiveness of this kind is also encountered in the non-material domain, in which belongs, for example, in sociology the behavior of whole groups, when they suddenly seem to be subject to an idea of a new kind, almost the mode or spiritual currents of a culture, a new direction in painting or a new stylistic turn in literature.[76]

But it is not only cultural phenomena that can be understood in accordance with this principle, but all knowledge, the grasping of a thought or, more precisely, the circumstance in which a thought, an idea, suddenly occurs to us.

> Just as in a puzzle, an entirely newly interconnected image comes before our eyes. In our brain there takes place a kind of phase transition in consciousness, and much that was previously unconnected suddenly appears as meaningfully ordered, troubled reflections

suddenly give way to the relief of certainty. This new knowledge had lain dormant in us, but suddenly it takes us over like an inspiration.[77]

Haken makes the following comment on this highly familiar phenomenon:

> One cannot resist the impression that similar processes are at work here as those we are familiar with in other domains of synergetics. A new order (that is, a new idea) arises through a fluctuation ('inspiration') which then successfully subordinates and correlates, or enslaves, individual aspects to itself. Again, however, all this happens fully through self-organization – even our thoughts organize themselves into new insights, new knowledge.[78]

Now, Schelling's characterisation of the fourth instance shows great structural similarity with the role of such a regulator. After a symmetry break between the three 'potencies' of pronominal, predicative and propositional being has been attained, their equipollence, as Schelling says, ceases to be, and the propositional model correspondingly gains the upper hand and 'enslaves' pronominal and predicative being, that is, forces them into a structurally compatible relation. Taken not in itself, but *in its role as 'regulator'*, propositional being is not already Schelling's fourth instance, but it is its 'actual' or 'active' document. *This fourth moment is therefore the sheer unity that every regulator exemplifies.* Only in reference to this One without properties does the chaos of rotary predication become capable of overcoming itself, that is, of otherwise independent self-organisation. Schelling puts exactly this point thus:

> Indeed, nature necessarily requires external assistance to the extent that nature only produces its wonders as an organic part of a higher whole. But allowing for this help, which only serves to posit nature in freedom, nature takes everything from out of itself and can be purely and completely explained simply from out of itself.[79]

What it is that, in natural processes, provides for the regulator being able to play any role whatever, Schelling calls its 'soul-like essence'. This expression, however, stands simply for something that indicates *susceptibility to unity*, for such susceptibility is presupposed by nature's self-organisation. This susceptibility ensures that all natural equipment remains in its way oriented towards unity per regulator, an orientation that Schelling calls *nature's longing*. The effect of unity is not an effect in the proper sense of a causal connection, but simply an attractive, *magical* one. The sheer being of the One exerts a magical, transformative effect on the rotary turbulence of the possible, to which, as though spellbound, it submits, that is, transitions into structures. This transition is the great crisis: the structure-negating potential energy of pronominal being and the energy-requiring structural potential of predicative being emerge from their spinning competition for supersession, step apart from one another and render the range of possibilities free for self-organising processes, for the emergence of the cosmos.

We may also, if we wish to follow Schelling here, ask, albeit not in the fullest sense, after the causes of the world's emergence, for this can only be in relations susceptible to causality. Here, regarding the origin of the world, there is manifestly only an incitation after the magical model. But here too, this is not an incitement of the magical *act*, but an incitement by enchantment in the sense of a fascination. The wild, pre-worldly whirl of predicative rotation will indeed escape the formless pressing in all its elements, but longing just to be what has being, so to speak, only by victory over its adversary. For suddenly,

> Through its simple presence, without any movement [...] that which is higher, magically, so to speak, rouses in that [eternally commencing] life, the yearning for freedom.[80]

In other passages, Schelling also speaks of an 'irresistible magic',[81] of 'bewitchment'.[82] He begins from the One, which he also calls 'the eternal freedom to be' or the 'will that wills nothing'. These expressions can only be understood when they are contrasted with what they stand out against, that is, from the necessity to be and a willing that wills something.

If something necessarily exists, it exists dependently upon determinants. This, however, is an index of a lacking autonomy [*Unselbständigkeit*]. The same goes for a will that wills something: it is the expression of dissatisfaction; something that desires something that it itself is not; it is the index of a lack. If we may speak at all of a One to which existence and will attach, then, insofar as the meaning of One is to be observed, there can be no consideration of a determined existence or of a will desiring something. Something that manifestly has the *choice* whether to be or not is not befitting of a determined existence; a will that wills nothing is something too much its own, lacking nothing. If we really want to fasten this One to the cross of these determinations, then it quietly becomes a living One, for how otherwise could it have the choice of whether to be or not, how otherwise could it be a self-sufficient will? Schelling also calls this autonomous and self-sufficient One 'that which is without nature, which eternal nature desires, is not a being and does not have being, although it is also not the opposite'.[83]

Ultimately, in the characterisation of this unique one, our language restlessly fails. We attempt to paraphrase it, but here we can grasp nothing correctly, and language slips away. This is really not surprising, since being susceptible to linguistic characterisation presupposes that we are also *a parte rei* [in reality] provided with characteristics, and this is precisely not the case with the meaning of the One: it is 'without character'. And Schelling quite beautifully adds: 'Taste, or, the gift of differentiation, finds nothing tasteful in the sublime, just as it finds little to taste in water that is scooped from the spring.'[84]

Thus, however we proceed linguistically here, our descriptions will be unable to produce more than deictic effects on this One without properties, and it cannot be surprising that not everyone will follow these hints. I would therefore like simply and further to consider that the undoubtedly diffuse meaning of the One cannot be removed by retreating to the definition of the numerical one. Since Frege,[85] we define this recourse to a definition by abstraction, by means of which we first define the concept of equinumerosity, in order then to introduce the cardinal number above the concept of Number.[86]

There is no doubt, however, that to define an intuitive understanding of equinumerosity, which can achieve even without counting, by means of unequivocal coordination (bijection) already draws on the meaning of the One, which is therefore always only documented by invariant [*identitätsfeste*] numerical magnitudes. So neither is it any wonder that Frege never got to the end of his reflections on one. Even at the end, in a diary entry from 25 March 1924, it remains an open question:

It is indeed progress when we no longer view number as a thing, but rather as something in a thing by which we maintain it possible that different things, despite their differences, have the same One in them, as different leaves can, say, have the same green in them. Now in what things do we find the One? Do we not have the One in each thing?[87]

What Frege has in mind here is indeed the identity relation (x) $(x = x)$, which ensures that we may replace 'thing' with 'something that is equal to itself'. But here too it must already be ensured that 'something' has a unitary meaning, that the variable x is univocal. Now, the variable does not denote or designate, but has, in Frege's terminology, no 'reference [*Bedeutung*]', but rather only 'indicates an object'.[88] Even with this indication of an object we already lay claim to the meaning of the One, a meaning therefore that will not be completely excavated by our understanding of the sign of relation '=', but is evidently found far below.

Perhaps it is the case that we would indeed have gained something for a philosophical understanding of the One if we were better informed about the essence of the variable. It secures universality for us, but at the cost of reference. Is there a law hidden behind this cost–benefit analysis? Must a maximal degree of universality be paid for straight away with the complete loss of every force, even if only indicative? A sign for everything that has absolutely no indicative force any longer? Schelling would answer here:

> It certainly is nothing, but in the way that pure freedom is nothing. It is like the will that wills nothing, that desires no object, for which all things are equal and is therefore moved by none of them. Such a will is nothing and everything. It is nothing insofar as it neither desires to become actual itself nor wants any kind of actuality. It is everything because only from it as eternal freedom comes all force and because it has all things under it, rules everything, and is ruled by nothing.[89]

That this orgy of metaphor is unavoidable by virtue of the material at issue, that therefore definitive limits of a reconstruction of *The Ages of the World*'s arguments are accumulating here too, neither can nor should be contested. We had simply to push the insight that we do not master these difficulties by ignoring them.

§ 19 Schelling's world formula

Schelling's *The Ages of the World* is not only a 'popularised' system of philosophy as the provisional gestalt of a future epic of the new age, but it also fights for an argument which, according to the claim, can only be characterised as a *world formula*. Schelling actually delivered such a formula in *The Ages of the World* which wants to decipher the symbolic summation of his calculated predication-theoretical speculations. However, one must not overestimate the claim that this formula can bear: it represents nothing more than a graphic stenogram of his speculation; it is nothing with which one could 'calculate', and without commentary it therefore remains meaningless. Schelling provides his world formula in the following graphic form:[90]

$$\left(\frac{A^3}{A^2 = (A = B)}\right)B$$

This so-called identity formula wants to be read like this: what is the same, if A = B, is A^2, and, *that* that is, is A^3; but this always stands in opposition to the fact that this relationship, the mode of presentation[91] of identity, is threatened by this itself (B). Therefore, expressed with Frege: there are only identity relations because there is sense [*Sinn*], but this is always just *the mode of presentation of identity*, and *not identity itself*, and it is nothing without it.[92] On the other hand, identity, without its mode of presentation, is utter nonsense, an object without a name or description, the semantic black hole, the pre-relational One. One can also interpret this formula in terms of self-consciousness, but the sense of this figure is perhaps also the following: according to how it is made, affirmation (A) and negation (B) are the *same* insofar as with every judgement we make a *choice* between opposing thoughts. When that choice is made, one has *an act*: for the recognition (A) of one thought is always *identical* with the rejection (B) of the contradictory opposite ($\bar{p}$). In this respect, (A = B) is valid. According to how it is made, affirmation and negation are therefore the same (= A^2), although what is affirmed and what is negated is something different (p and $\bar{p}$).

Hence, the sameness of how it is done and the dissimilarity of the judged belong together in every judgement, and the proposition

(A^3) documents this togetherness, to which the judgement is taken [$A^2 = (A = B)$]. These judgements are epistemically *everything down to one*, that is, they have their directive ontically outside of themselves. Judgement thereby *experiences* the One as the negation of the arbitrariness of what can be judged. Only through this external, that is, the negation of arbitrariness that precedes predication, the unitarian obligation, is there something like 'validity'. The true is the whole down to one, and for this the B stands outside the parentheses. The predication-theoretical reading is one with the cosmological meaning. For whatever energies allow the cosmos to take shape, they ultimately feed on a *monotropism of chaos* that cannot be explained from it alone. It is only through the attractor of the One that it comes to symmetry breaks and phase transitions, to the genesis of a self-organising universe. It accordingly illustrates the 'negative force' symbolised here by B as

> a fire which draws Being into itself and which hence makes what is drawn in completely one with this force. It was totality and unity, but now both are fused into a single being. What is attracted or withdrawn is eternal nature, the totality. What attracts or draws is singular. Hence the whole can be designated in the following illustration:

$$\left(\frac{A^3}{A^2 = (A = B)}\right) B$$

This is the One and the Many (ἓν καὶ πᾶν) in intimate connection.[93]

However, I doubt whether this formula offers the reader any help with an understanding of Schelling's intuition worth mentioning. For its arithmetic *façon* makes access to its meaning more difficult than it facilitates it. Schelling's intuition here seems to be the following: however strong the self-organising force of the universe may be internally, it has the insurmountable weakness that it remains externally dependent on something that did not 'enslave' its competitors but rather itself, that is, on a self-contracting force, namely, the One. The suction of this self-contraction – the suction of the One – makes the frenzy of the antagonistic forces first able to organise itself (as marshal). The same goes for an epistemological reading: however strongly we develop our epistemic forces internally, they have a weakness that cannot be removed, namely, they remain external. This means they are initially and finally dependent on the One, which they do not produce themselves, but to which they are simply 'attracted' in synthesising accomplishments; through such accomplishments, they always just take advantage of the force of this attraction and thus document it. With this formula, Schelling therefore at least indicates that the dimension of the genesis of a constant supply of energy is required in order to remain 'open'. This energy supplies the original negation. Put differently: Schelling emphasises that the singular *Unum* [one] is the alpha and the omega. The alpha: it is what has always come before elementary predication; the omega: it remains independent with respect to all predication, 'a thing that nobody can fully think through'. The entire semantic corpus has ontic singularity outside of it. And only because that is the case are there phase transitions, is the semantic corpus at all capable of self-organisation and is there knowing and amplifications in knowing. Pronominal being cannot be predicatively or propositionally redeemed and this means that *semantic idealism shipwrecks on pronominal being.* Something whatever is the pre-rational spine of the rational. There is only sense [*Sinn*] because there is madness [*Wahnsinn*], affirmation only because of negation, consistency only because of inconsistency, consciousness only because there is unconsciousness. These relationships always say as much as negation is the *past* of affirmation; it is what had to pass to have been able to obtain thereby the affirmed reality. Affirmation is first possible through the repression of negation: *omnis determinatio est negatio praeterita* [all determination is a negation of the past]. Schelling illustrates this with a psychological example ('to get started with something'):

> The decision that would make any kind of act into a true beginning may not be brought before consciousness. It may not be *recalled*, which rightly means as much as taking it back. Whoever reserves it to themselves again and again to bring a decision to light never makes a beginning.[94]

The general sum of these relationships is then drawn in the following passage: 'the beginning does not know itself as such. Which really means: it may not know itself as a beginning. In the very beginning, nothing is or discerns itself as merely ground or beginning.'[95] This means: the beginning is blind; from the perspective of the matter itself, it is always what is first, but from the perspective of the concept, it is always what is later. It has become seeing and it has passed. Everything, everything that has taken on form and everything that exists rests on this past. Everything rests, as long as it exists, on a beginning that 'that never ceases to be a beginning'.[96]

That a beginning never ceases to be a beginning means something exists. And this means there is time. That something exists means in this context: something else no longer exists, although it exists as something that no longer exists, that is, as beginning. This remains 'repressed' in everything that exists. *Time is the mode of presentation of the beginning as repressed.* The original unity of the blind wanting remains repressed in every structure that arises, only to perish in the self-organisation of nature. Schelling expresses this thus: 'But since unity no longer has the antithesis outside of itself, but rather is united with it and it can no longer go out as the free, silent unity, it, so to speak, feels as if it were dying.'[97] Schelling also calls this *natural Golgotha* 'bitterness which is, nay, must be, the interior of all life, and which immediately erupts whenever it is not soothed'.[98] This 'source of bitterness', 'the profound discontent that lies in all life', 'this poison of life',[99] is precisely what Schelling in another passage designates, anticipating Adorno's negative aesthetics, as the art-object:

> One often speaks of the charm of nature for humans, but the most exquisite charm that nature has for humans is that *melancholy*, which poured out over them. It is, so to speak, a silent reproach for humans, that melancholy whose sweet poison the artist and poet must understand how to suck from it if they want to arouse interest.[100]

But as remarkable as this aesthetic conception of a melancholy countenance of nature (Alanus: *planctus naturae*)[101] is (and it is remarkable if one formulates Schelling's counter-discourse to Hegel's discourse of the beautiful as the sensuous appearance [*Scheinen*] of the Idea as follows: the beautiful is the sensuous appearance of the *distress of the Idea*), the persevering process of repression in all forms indicates nothing less than a permanent threat to the existence of the universe, its looming implosion, a threat 'of universal destruction, of the dissolution of things again into chaos'.[102] It seems that the insight into this internal threat to the universe, which is simultaneously the condition of its genesis, was Schelling's motivating experience during the period of *The Ages of the World*. It was a course he could no longer evade. He therefore may have wondered about idealistic, nay, pantheistic attempts at harmonisation, believing that there was something consolatory in them, that the unity is in everything: 'But were they capable of penetrating the exterior surface of things, they would see that the true prime matter of all life and existence is precisely what is horrifying.'[103]

One must bring to mind in graphic vividness the exorbitance of this experience, which also symbolises Schelling's world formula, to obtain an inkling of his convulsion, which releases an ideational quake, of which the fragments of *The Ages of the World* are the seismograph. They register 'vibrations' that far exceed the scale of what is epistemically bearable for humans. We would say today that the centre of this quake is the insight into a fundamental inconsistency, which remains a lurking ground in all consistent relationships, a thought which cannot really be grasped and is an epistemic impertinence. It is therefore no wonder that the presentation of this initial inconsistency demands enormous linguistic efforts, which leave behind everything argumentative and to a certain extent only offer an evocative support for its understanding. In the passages where philosophical discourse explodes in an orgiastic figurativeness, Schelling demonstrates a power of speech to which there is nothing comparable in the whole of philosophy.

An example of this is Schelling's description of the internal syndromes of genesis, the self-birth of a whole from nature and spirit in an excited jostling between the energies of inconsistency (the blind will) and consistency (pure unity). The scene is arranged so that the inconsistent energies are stimulated by the consistent energies, with the effect that the beginning autism of the blind willing, attempting to be consistent by itself in order to extirpate pure consistency, is broken. These attempts at consistency are the products of an auto-epistemic universe, a model of self-organisation that we can recognise. With Schelling this reads – incomparably – like this:

> The acting potency does not express itself immediately with full power but rather as a faint attracting, like that which precedes the arousal from a deep slumber. With increasing might, the forces in Being are aroused to dull and blind action. Powerful and, because the gentle unity of the spirit is alien to Being, formless, births arise.

No longer in that state of interiority or clairvoyance nor enraptured by blessed visions that portend the future, what exists in this conflict struggles as if in grave dreams which arise out of the past because they arise out of Being. Anxiety is the governing affect that corresponds to the conflict of directions in Being, since it does not know whether to go in or out. Meanwhile, the orgasm of forces increases more and more and lets the contracting force fear utter cision and complete dissolution. But while the contracting force releases its life and, so to speak, discerns itself as already past, the higher form of its being and the silent purity of spirit rise before it like lightening. But this purity, in contrast to the blindly contracting will, is the essential unity in which freedom, the intellect, and differentiation dwell. Hence, the will, while contracting, would like to grasp the lightening flash of freedom and make it its own in order to thereby become a freely creating and conscious will. It would then get out of loathing and, overcoming the conflict of forces, communicate to its creations the essential unity that is intellect, spirit, and beauty. But the blind will cannot grasp gentle freedom. Rather, freedom is for the will an overwhelming and incomprehensible spirit and that is why the will is frightened by the appearances of spirit. The will no doubt feels that the spirit is the will's true being and, despite the spirit's gentleness, that it is stronger than the will in its severity. At the sight of that spirit, the will becomes as if insensate and seeks blindly to grasp spirit and to copy it inwardly in what the will produces, as if it could somehow keep a firm hold on spirit. But the will only acts as if with an alien intellect over which it has no command. This intellect is an intermediary between the utter night of consciousness and levelheaded spirit.

Everything stems from these enlightenments that, e.g., is something intelligible and ordered in the structure of the universe, by virtue of which the universe actually appears to be the external figure of an indwelling spirit.[104]

The genesis, according to this portrayal, is a single great attempt by inconsistent energies to expunge mimetically pure consistency. Since this does not succeed, we just have a universe halfway between inconsistency and consistency. This applies to us, we earthlings who have made the most progress on this path. That is, in plain language: bombarded by inconsistent energies, the human spirit also organises itself into consistent patterns that we call knowledge. Schelling in turn analysed with unprecedented radicalism the syndrome of this mental self-organisation, which, without inconsistent energies and without whose orientation towards pure consistency, would immediately collapse.

§ 20 Reason and madness

For all the difficulty of reconstructing *The Ages of the World*, its speculative objective is utterly beyond doubt: namely, to provide proof that throughout the genesis of the universe pulse both affirmative and negative, both rational and irrational energies:

> At its first genesis, the structure of the universe clearly enough shows the presence of an inner, spiritual potency. But the contribution and auxiliary influence of an unreasonable (irrational) principle that could only be delimited, but never overwhelmed, is just as unmistakable.[105]

What goes for the universe as a whole is equally valid for our mental constitution. It too is fired up by unconscious, ultimately inconsistent energies, which we harness by orienting them towards consistency. Precisely this is the hard labour of a mind that must 'pull itself together' in order to become itself, to be and to persist. But it was not always thus. Only when the binding of instincts is concluded, allowing an orientation towards Something whatever in the organisation of information processing to flash up; only then will the energies required for the mind's labour be roused. This work is not accomplished at a stroke, the focused force does not grow immediately out of the dissipation of inconsistent energies. In the transitional field from not-meaning to meaning, shoots of meaning appear in amorphous masses of not-meaning, generating a plasm of madness, from which alone reason may result.

The phase prior to the emergence of rationality is Dionysian for Schelling. Here again he outlines a dramatic image, which completely anticipates Nietzsche's fundamental ideas:

> The ancients did not speak in vain of a divine and holy madness. We even see nature, in the process of its free unfolding, becoming, in proportion to its approach to spirit, ever more, so to speak, frenzied. No doubt, all things of nature are found in an insensate state. But we see those creatures that belong to the time of the last struggle between cision and unification, consciousness and unconsciousness, and that immediately precede humanity among the creations of nature, walking about in a state similar to drunkenness. Panthers or tigers do not pull the carriage of Dionysus in vain. For this wild frenzy of inspiration in which nature found itself when it

was in view of the being was celebrated in the nature worship of prescient ancient peoples by the drunken festivals of Bacchic orgies. Furthermore, that inner self-laceration of nature, that wheel of initial birth spinning about itself as if mad, and the terrible forces of the annular drive operating within this wheel, are depicted in other frightful splendors of the primeval customs of polytheistic worship by acts of self-flaying rage. One such act was auto-castration (which was done in order to express either the unbearable quality of the oppressive force or its cessation as a procreative potency). There was also the carrying about of the dismembered parts of a lacerated God, or the insensate, raving dances, or the shocking procession of the mother of all gods on the carriage with iron wheels, accompanied by the din of a coarse music that is partly deafening and partly lacerating. For nothing is more similar to that inner madness than music, which, through the incessant eccentric relinquishing and re-attracting of tones, most clearly imitates that primordial movement. Music itself is a turning wheel that, going out from a single point, always, through all excesses, spins back again to the beginning.[106]

Now, we might think that, with the overcoming of the birth phase of human reason and its Dionysian spring sacrifices of the spirit, the phase of madness is put behind us. According to Schelling, however, this view, which we nowadays want to render harmless, is, as cannot otherwise be supposed, completely erroneous. For the original madness here at issue is the *mantic* presupposition for the emergence of a *semantically* self-organising consciousness[107] and remains, as this presupposition, the effective energetic source of its merely dissipative structure, which for precisely that reason remains permanently endangered. Finally, then, there are two mental constitutions that are constructed over this original madness:

> There is one kind of person that governs madness and precisely in this overwhelming shows the highest force of the intellect. The other kind of person is governed by madness and is someone who really is mad. One cannot say, strictly speaking, that madness originates in them. It only comes forth as something that is always there (for without continuous solicitation of it, there would be no consciousness)…[108]

With this conception of a pre-epistemic madness, Schelling appears in the ancient tradition.[109] But the epistemological point of this conception is only evident when we consider what informational surplus secures precisely these components of madness for our mental constitution. Namely, it preconceives the entire semantic dimension that consciousness makes its own and maintains a connection with something that only ever lays claim to, but does not itself generate, this dimension: orientation towards anything whatever. This 'mad' mantic resource is something that enables us to be oriented towards unity when we wish to arrange our semantic relations univocally. Because via this effort towards order we are always to some extent semantically prejudiced, this deeper lying mantic resource seldom comes into view: 'Being posited in oneself' hinders the person. 'Being posited outside of oneself helps one, as our language magnificently indicates.'[110]

What Schelling saw here absolutely cannot be overestimated as regards its epistemological significance. For this pre-epistemic ecstatic component of madness provides not only the foundations for an entirely new understanding for what it means that something exists, but also quite clearly focuses Schelling's going beyond Kant. I will first recapitulate the arguments concerning the understanding of existence in thetic form.

The traditional theory:

1. The decision regarding whether a predicate F holds true of something, that is, that there exists an x of the kind that $(\exists x)$ (Fx) is true for at least one argument a, does not issue in the predicate F, but a research strategy informed by the predicate F.
2. Existence determining research strategies represent the epistemic meaning of existence. This consists in the information on *what* is being researched, *how* it is researched and terminates in a protocol as to *whether* we have made a discovery.
3. The epistemic meaning of existence is summarised in the thesis that being is not a real predicate (Kant), but a second order predicate or a property of predication (Frege).

Schelling's ecstatic concept of existence:

1. In the fullest sense, the circumstance *that* something exists is not dependent on there being definition procedures or research strategies that give us information as to *whether* something

exists. Existence is epistemically neutral. Put differently: the meaning of being extends further than the semantic organisation of the scope of our research. We are in principle ready to admit that something possibly exists for which we have no predicates at our disposal, that we cannot linguistically express in descriptions, but at most only indicate by pronomina (Something whatever).

2. That we are informed about the meaning of being transcending the semantic dimension at all presupposes that we may somehow lay claim to what lies outside the scope of semantics. We may already in principle lay this claim through our sensibility. By it, we always experience more than we could characterise semantically. But we also need to lay claim to the outer reaches of the sensible dimension, since we are in principle equally prepared to concede that the meaning of being reaches far further than our senses.

3. The question is therefore how do we hold a claim to the sphere that lies outside what is semantically and sensuously characterisable? A claim that must be available to us, although the meaning of being will be irreducible to what can be semantically or sensuously characterised. Schelling's answer here draws on an anthropological resource: we are, in our mental constitution, in a fundamental sense always *outside* the semantic and sensible sphere, *inside* which we forge our identities. That is, clearly stated: we are in a profound sense factically *outside ourselves*, in order that we may *come to ourselves* at all. Being outside oneself implies a kind of experience that we always require if we wish to lend meaning to the subject-independency of our validity claims. The same goes for our understanding of existence. That something exists means, accordingly, to exist independently of existential determinations. And this means: to be is ultimately not a property of a thing, not a property of predicates; rather, to be is to be a property, albeit a property of the world. But not even this exhausts the meaning of being, if indeed the world arose. Ultimately, this says: being is a property of something that is not a thing, not a predicate, not a world, nor a property at all, but an existential condition of everything that is sufficient by itself. The self-sufficiency of the existential condition of all is the object of *The Ages of the World*.

We must always take it into account that Schelling does not claim to explain a meaning of being that can be conceptually determined, but rather one upon which every determination of this kind is already dependent. We must already know what it means *that* something exists if we wish to investigate *whether* there are *F*'s, for example. The difficulties in discussing existence in a predicate-free space are naturally considerable, because we must operate with a type of experience that preconceives the entire scope of our reason. In the *Philosophy of Revelation*, Schelling formulated this so:

> Reason can posit what has being in which there is still nothing of a concept, of a whatness, only as something that is posited absolutely *outside itself* (of course only in order to acquire it thereafter, *a posteriori*, as its content, and in this way to return to itself at the same time). In this positing, reason is therefore set outside itself, absolutely ecstatic.[111]

This pre-rational meaning of being, this ecstatic 'concept' of existence, deals with something that existed prior to all conceptuality, and which must therefore be certified not as non-conceptual, but as free of all concepts, purely empirical. The type of this pure empiricism is here the ecstasy of reason in its pronominal reference to anything whatever. Schelling himself says that these considerations are otherwise fully compatible with an interpretation free of theology:

> In the positive philosophy, therefore, I do not proceed from the concept of God, as the ontological argument and the former metaphysics had attempted to do. Rather, I must do away with precisely this concept, the concept of *God*, in order to proceed from that which just exists, in which nothing at all is thought other than just that which just exists…[112]

Schelling's ecstatic concept of existence doubtless blows up Kant's critically restricted concept of reason. But Schelling nevertheless sets great store by demonstrating the compatibility of his reflections with Kant's critical results, so as to be, on this point, *still an orthodox Kantian where he goes far beyond him.*

According to Kant, the ideal of pure reason, the sum total of all possibility, is nothing of which we may rightly affirm that it exists, if indeed we do not wish to fall into the trap of a subreptive use of reason,[113] as for example was typical of the dogmatic philosophy. The subreptive use of reason occurs when, from mere ideas (soul, God, world), we infer something existing that corresponds to them. In this inference we transcend the limits of a certifiable use of reason, that is, one designed for the mere regulation of our continuing cognitive efforts. Such a transcending by inferring something existent that corresponds to the ideas generates only the delusive appearance of knowledge. Schelling too subscribes to this critical restriction on our application of reason. Yet he nevertheless does not want to deny existence to the transcendental ideal. How can this work? Primarily, of course, only so that we do not arrogate to ourselves the capacity to *infer* something existing from the concept of the idea alone and to which that idea corresponds. Such an inference is in fact, according to Schelling, illegitimately transcendent. What we require, therefore, is an experience that has already anticipated all concepts, an experience therefore that already puts us outside the semantic dimension, so that we do not really need to transcend this, but must only see to it that we are able to return again to this semantic dimension. If there is such an experience, then the problem is not transcendence, but descendence: 'positive philosophy', he says, is '*philosophia descendens* (descending from above)'.[114]

What would such an experience, always already putting us outside the semantic dimension along with something that exists and that only exists, that is, without a predicatively definable restriction (as F), look like? This experience must at least be of such a kind that we have it only when we are outside ourselves, not with ourselves, but with Something whatever. Schelling conceives this experience as madness, ecstasy, but these dramatic turns of phrase are only drastic terms for the elementary experience that we are when we make reference to something that is not with us, but rather with something else. This is a sub-semantic reference, that is, of the mantic kind. And we must add: we are first in something else and are only then with ourselves.

With this option of an original outer being from which alone we grow into ourselves, Schelling is the first, like Martin Heidegger and Gilbert Ryle later, to blow up the foundations of the imprisoning Cartesian theory of consciousness that still continues in Kant's commitment to the immanence of reason. Ryle provided a highly popular illustration of the Cartesian theory:

> The beloved but spurious question, 'How can a person get beyond his sensations to apprehension of external realities?' is often posed as if the situation were like this. There is immured in a windowless cell a prisoner, who has lived there in solitary confinement since birth. All that comes to him from the outside world is flickers of light thrown upon his cell-walls and tappings heard through the stones; yet from these observed flashes and tappings he becomes, or seems to become, apprised of unobserved football-matches, flower-gardens, and eclipses of the sun. How then does he learn the ciphers in which his signals are arranged, or even find out that there are such things as ciphers?[115]

For Ryle, this theory is just a variation of the category mistakes of the type mind as ghost in the machine. Heidegger summarises the phenomenal fund (by which Ryle may well have been inspired) that speaks against the Cartesian theory, thus:

> When Dasein directs itself towards something and grasps it, it does not somehow first get out of an inner sphere in which it has been proximally encapsulated, but its primary kind of Being is such that it is always 'outside' alongside entities which it encounters and which belong to a world already discovered.[116]

The theory of this 'primary kind of Being' ultimately provides Heidegger, directly inheriting Schelling's intuition, with an analysis of the ecstatic horizon of Dasein from which it first reverts to the objectification of things:

> [F]actical Dasein, understanding itself and its world ecstatically in the unity of the 'there', comes back from these horizons to the entities encountered within them. Coming back to these entities understandingly is the existential meaning of letting them be encountered by making them present; that is why we call them entities 'within the world'.[117]

Heidegger's theory is not to be debated here. It is important that Schelling already had precisely the intuition that we are always already in a certain sense outside the semantic dimension, with *Something whatever that exists*, from which alone we always come back to determinate things that exist. Since that with which we always already are is nothing predicative or conceptual in itself, is nothing that we can first *infer*, starting from concepts, this already-being-with-something-that-exists is not something that Kant's critique addresses. This is precisely how Schelling argues:

> If I infer from the *idea* of the most supreme being its *existence*, this is [an illegitimate, W.H.] transcending: I first posited the idea and now wish to pass from it over into existence – here is then a transcendence [illegitimate, W.H.]. If, however, I *proceed* from that which is anterior to all concepts, then I have surpassed nothing, and, on the contrary, if one calls this being transcendent and I advance within it to its concept, then I have surpassed the transcendent and *in this way* again become immanent [...] Kant forbade metaphysics transcendence, but he forbade it only for dogmatizing reason, that is, for reason that of itself seeks, by means of inferences, to reach existence; he did not forbid reason to proceed conversely from that which *simply* and, thus, infinitely *exists* to the concept of the most supreme *being* as *posterius* (he had not thought of it, for this possibility had not even presented itself to him).[118]

We do not, at any rate, need to engage with this concept of the most supreme being. It is sufficient that the reference to an existence without predicates, to Something whatever that exists, is secured. But this reference must be secured, because otherwise we would have none, that is, nor would we have any predicative reference to objects, for we would then have no understanding at our disposal of anything whatever, and without this understanding there would be no understanding of anything determinate. This reference to Something whatever that exists is also operative in every definite predication, and indeed simply in the so-called quantification of existence, that is, in inferring from Fa to $(\exists x)(Fx)$. The quantification of existence is the predicative, rational echo of our non-predicative, pre-rational reference to Something whatever that exists.

Along these lines, Schelling's speculation remains even today a metaphysical theory open to discussion, in proceeding *from* and in coming back *to* a theory of predication and reference. It appears that we must study his philosophy anew, at the very least from this perspective. And the issue of this effort will doubtless be some variant of Plato's remarkable sentence, which even today has not yet been understood: 'the greatest of blessings comes to us through madness'.[119] After Plato, only Schelling understood, with unexampled radicality, that *apophantic*, truth-apt *logos* refers to an *apomantic psyche*[120] that is outside itself, and that, despite all the theological licence in which his speculations are embedded – *perhaps simply to be able to bear them* – there always remains something bewildering about them. *Where danger threatens, that which saves from it also grows*, as Hölderlin formulates the maxim of a metaphysical solace.[121] Schelling is convinced of the opposite: *where what saves is, danger also grows*.

Notes

1. [SW I/8, 199; *Ages*, xxxv.]
2. [SW I/8, 199; *Ages*, xxxv.]
3. [SW I/8, 200; *Ages*, xxxvi. See the translator's note 5 to this complex sentence in *Ages*, 136.]
4. [SW I/8, 205; *Ages*, xxxix.]
5. [SW I/8, 213; *Ages*, 8.]
6. [SW I/8, 213; *Ages*, 8.]
7. [SW I/8, 214; *Ages*, 8.]
8. [SW I/8, 214; *Ages*, 8.]
9. Cf. above, §§ 12–13.
10. Cf. *Weltalter*, 28–9 (Draft I [*Ages 1811*, 86–7) and 128–9 (Draft II [*Ages 1813*, 129–30]).
11. *Weltalter*, 194. [This passage is found in the section of Schröter's edition of the *Weltalter* entitled 'Outlines and Fragments for the First Book of *The Ages of the World*', and belongs to what the editor calls the 'Earliest Table of Concepts' – tr.]
12. *Philosophie der Offenbarung 1841/42* (Paulus-Nachschrift), ed. Manfred Frank (Frankfurt am Main: Suhrkamp, 1977), 101. [Trans. Klaus Ottmann, *F.W.J. Schelling: Philosophy of Revelation (1841–1842) and Related Texts* (Thompson, CT: Spring, 2020), 44–5 – tr.]
13. [SW I/8, 217; *Ages*, 10.]
14. [SW I/8, 217; *Ages*, 10.]
15. [Cf. here SW I/8, 210; *Ages*, 5f.]
16. [SW I/8, 211; *Ages*, 6.]
17. [SW I/8, 212; *Ages*, 7.]
18. [SW I/8, 212; *Ages*, 7.]
19. [SW I/8, 216; *Ages*, 10.]
20. [SW I/8, 216; *Ages*, 10.]
21. [SW I/8, 219; *Ages*, 12.]
22. [SW I/8, 219; *Ages*, 13.]
23. [SW I/8, 218; *Ages*, 11. Bracketed comments are interpolated by the author.]
24. [SW I/8, 220; *Ages*, 13.]
25. [SW I/8, 224; *Ages*, 16.]
26. [SW I/8, 224; *Ages*, 16.]
27. [SW I/8, 224; *Ages*, 16.]
28. [SW I/8, 225; *Ages*, 16.]
29. [SW I/8, 227; *Ages*, 18.]
30. [SW I/8, 227; *Ages*, 18.]

31. [SW I/8, 228; *Ages*, 19.]
32. [SW I/8, 228; *Ages*, 19.]
33. [SW I/8, 228–9; *Ages*, 19.]
34. [Cf. SW I/8, 229; *Ages*, 20; SW I/8, 231n; *Ages*, 21 n.4.]
35. [SW I/8, 229; *Ages*, 20.]
36. [SW I/8, 229; *Ages*, 20.]
37. [SW I/8, 229–30; *Ages*, 19–20.]
38. [SW I/8, 230; *Ages*, 20.]
39. [Cf. *Weltalter*, 218: 'O past, you abyss of thought! (*O Vergangenheit, du Abgrund der Gedanken!*').]
40. [SW I/8, 232; *Ages*, 21.]
41. [*Weltalter*, 218; *Ages 1811*, 200.]
42. [Hugo von Hofmannsthal, *Weltgeheimnis*, 'Der tiefe Brunnen weiß es wohl; / In den gebückt, begriffs ein Mann, / Begriff es und verlor es dann. / Und redet irr' und sang ein Lied—. 'World-Secret', in *The Lyrical Poems of Hugo von Hofmannsthal*, trans. Charles Wharton Stock (New Haven, CT: Yale University Press, 1918), 32.]
43. On this, see my destruction of epistemic nihilism in Nietzsche, in *Destruktion des epistemischen Nihilismus bei Nietzsche*, in Wolfram Hogrebe, *Deutsche Philosophie im XIX. Jahrhundert* (Munich: Wilhelm Fink, 1987), 174ff.
44. [SW I/8, 207; *Ages*, 3.]
45. [SW I/8, 229; *Ages*, 20.]
46. [SW I/8, 231; *Ages*, 21.]
47. [SW I/8, 266; *Ages*, 47.]
48. [SW I/8, 232; *Ages*, 21.]
49. [SW I/8, 232; *Ages*, 22 citing Petronius, *Satyricon*, 119.]
50. *Zur Geschichte der neueren Philosophie: Münchner Vorlesungen* (1827) [SW I/10, 102; *On the History of Modern Philosophy*, trans. Andrew Bowie (Cambridge: Cambridge University Press, 1994), 116.]
51. *Theaetetus* 183b. Cf., for this, Wolfram Hogrebe, *Archäologische Bedeutungspostulate* [*Archeological Postulates of Meaning*] (Freiburg and Munich: Alber, 1977), § 16, 197.
52. In the above cited Munich lectures (*On the History of Modern Philosophy*), Schelling refers to the teaching in ancient logic of the *termini reduplicatavi*: 'In the older logic this kind of positing, where A is not posited *simpliciter* but *as* A, was called "reduplicative" or *reduplicatio*' [SW I/10, 103; *On the History of Modern Philosophy*, 117].
53. [SW I/8, 232; *Ages*, 22.]
54. [SW I/8, 234; *Ages*, 23.]
55. [SW I/8, 238; *Ages*, 27.]
56. *Politeia* [*Republic*] 509b.
57. [SW I/8, 232; *Ages*, 22.]
58. [SW I/8, 240; *Ages*, 28. Bracketed comments are interpolated by the author.]
59. [SW I/8, 241; *Ages*, 29.]
60. [SW I/8, 243; *Ages*, 31.]
61. [SW I/8, 247; *Ages*, 33.]
62. [SW I/8, 253; *Ages*, 37.]
63. [SW I/8, 256; *Ages*, 40.]
64. [SW I/8, 258; *Ages*, 42.]

65. [SW I/8, 259; *Ages*, 42.]
66. [SW I/8, 259; *Ages*, 42.]
67. [SW I/8, 261; *Ages*, 44.]
68. [SW I/8, 253; *Ages*, 38. Cf. also SW I/8, 324; *Ages*, 92–3.]
69. [SW I/8, 263; *Ages*, 45.]
70. [SW I/8, 263; *Ages*, 45.]
71. [Cf. SW I/8, 239; *Ages*, 28.]
72. [Cf.,SW I/8, 239; *Ages*, 28.]
73. [Cf. SW I/8, 268; *Ages*, 49.]
74. Hermann Haken, *Erfolgsgeheimnisse der Natur* (Stuttgart: Deutsche Verlags Anstalt, 1981), 20ff. and *passim* [trans. Fred Bradley, *The Science of Structure: Synergetics* (New York: Van Nostrand Reinhold, 1984). Haken, emeritus professor of theoretical physics in the University of Stuttgart, is the founder of synergetics – tr.] That Schelling's thought acquires a surprising contemporaneity from the conceptual perspective of the theory of dynamics for open systems is attested to for his nature-philosophy by the work of Marie-Luise Heuser-Keßler, *Die Produktivität der Natur: Schellings Naturphilosohpie und das neue Paradigma der Selbstorganisation in der Naturwissenschaften* (Berlin: Duncker and Humblot, 1986).
75. Haken, *Erfolgsgeheimnisse der Natur*, 19.
76. Ibid., 21.
77. Ibid., 195.
78. Ibid., 195–6.
79. [SW I/8, 276–7; *Ages*, 56–7.]
80. [SW I/8, 239; *Ages*, 27–8.]
81. [SW I/8, 277; *Ages*, 56.]
82. [SW I/8, 280; *Ages*, 59.]
83. [SW I/8, 236; *Ages*, 25.]
84. [SW I/8, 235; *Ages*, 24.]
85. Gottlob Frege, *The Foundations of Arithmetic*, §§ 66ff. [Part trans. in Michael Beaney (ed.), *The Frege Reader* (Oxford: Blackwell, 1997), pp. 113ff. We have followed Beaney rather than Austin in translating Frege's *gleichzahlig* as 'equinumerous' in place of Austin's 'misleading' (so Beaney, 113n) rendering of it as merely 'equal' – tr.]
86. [Following Austin and Beaney, Frege's *Anzahl* is translated as 'Number', leaving 'number' for *Zahl*. Cf. Beaney (ed.), *The Frege Reader*, 91n.]
87. Gottlob Frege, *Posthumous Writings*, trans. Peter Long and Roger White (Oxford: Blackwell, 1984), 264.
88. Frege, *Basic Laws of Arithmetic*, § 17, trans. Philip A. Ebert, Marcus Rossberg, Crispin Wright and Roy T. Cook (Oxford: Oxford University Press, 2013), 31.
89. [SW I/8, 235; *Ages*, 24.]
90. [SW I/8, 235; *Ages*, 84.]
91. [It has become customary to translate Gottlob Frege's phrase, from 'Über Sinn und Bedeutung', '*die Art des Gegebenseins*', the way of being given, as 'the mode of presentation'. (Cf. pp. 26–7 in the standard pagination, established by the original appearance of Frege's article, 'Über Sinn und Bedeutung', *Zeitschrift für Philosophie und philosophische Kritik* NF 100 (1892), 25–50.) We have retained this translation because of its customary familiarity.]

92. [Cf. Frege, 'Über Sinn und Bedeutung', 26: 'Eine Verschiedenheit kann nur dadurch zu Stande kommen, daß der Unterschied des Zeichens einem Unterschiede in der Art des Gegebenseins des Bezeichneten entspricht.']
93. [SW I/8, 312; *Ages*, 84.]
94. [SW I/8, 314; *Ages*, 85.]
95. [SW I/8, 314; *Ages*, 86.]
96. [SW I/8, 314; *Ages*, 85.]
97. [SW I/8, 319; *Ages*, 89.]
98. [SW I/8, 319; *Ages*, 89.]
99. [Cf. SW I/8, 319; *Ages*, 89.]
100. *Grundlegung der positiven Philosophie: Münchener Vorlesung WS 1832/33 und SS 1833* [*Grounding of the Positive Philosophy: Munich Lectures, Winter Semester 1832/33 and Summer Semester 1833*], ed. Horst Fuhrmans (Turin: Bottega d'Erasmo, 1972), 479–80.
101. [The 'plaint of nature' is an allusion to the French poet-theologian Allain de Lille (*Alanus ab Insulis*), c. 1128–1202/03.]
102. [SW I/8, 329; *Ages*, 97.]
103. [SW I/8, 339; *Ages*, 104.]
104. [SW I/8, 336–7; *Ages*, 101–2.]
105. [SW I/8, 328; *Ages*, 95.]
106. [SW I/8, 337–8; *Ages*, 102–3.]
107. [Hogrebe offers a full account of the pre-semantic, or 'mantic' domain, in *Metaphysik und Mantik* [*Metaphysics and Mantics*] (Frankfurt am Main: Suhrkamp, 1992).]
108. [SW I/8, 339; *Ages*, 103–4.]
109. On this, see E. R. Dodds, *The Greeks and the Irrational* (Berkeley, CA: University of California Press, 1951).
110. [SW I/8, 296; *Ages*, 71.]
111. [SW II/3, 162–3, trans. Bruce Matthews, *Grounding of Positive Philosophy: The Berlin Lectures* (hereafter *Grounding*) (Albany, NY: State University of New York Press, 2007), 202-3. Translation slightly modified to accord with *Ages*.]
112. [SW II/3, 158; *Grounding*, 200.] Schelling continues here: 'to see whether the divine is to be reached from it. Thus, I cannot really prove the existence of God (whereby I somehow proceed from the concept of *God*), and the only concept given to me is of that which precedes all potency and, therefore, indubitably exists.'
113. [On the subreptive use of reason, see Kant, *CPR* A643/B671: 'We are entitled … to suppose that transcendental ideas have their own […] immanent use, although, when their meaning is misunderstood, and they are taken for concepts of real things, they become transcendent in their application and for that very reason can be delusive […] All [such] errors of subreption are to be ascribed to a defect of judgment, never to understanding or to reason.']
114. [SW II/3, 151n; *Grounding* 196n.]
115. Gilbert Ryle, *The Concept of Mind* (Harmondsworth: Penguin, 1963), 212.
116. Martin Heidegger, *Being and Time*, trans. John Macquarrie and Edward Robinson (Oxford: Blackwell, 1962), § 13, H.89.
117. Ibid., § 69, H.366.
118. [SW II/3, 169–70; *Grounding*, 208–9.]
119. *Phaedrus* 244a, trans. H. N. Fowler (Cambridge, MA: Harvard University Press, 1969).

120. Plato, *Republic*, trans. Paul Shorey (Cambridge, MA: Harvard University Press, 1963), 505e ['That, then, which every soul pursues and for its sake does all that it does, with an intuition of its reality, yet baffled and unable to apprehend its nature adequately, or to attain to any stable belief about it as about other things' – tr.]. Cf. here Wolfram Hogrebe, 'Eindeutigkeit und Vieldeutigkeit: Vorzüge einer indiskreten Ontologie' ['Monosemia and Polysemia: The Superiority of an Indiscrete Ontology'], in *Akten des 14. Deutschen Kongresses für Philosophie* (1987). [See also Hogrebe, *Metaphysik und Mantik*, §§ 17–22 – tr.]
121. ['Wo Gefahr ist, wächst das Rettende auch'. Hölderlin, *Patmos*, trans. Michael Hamburger, in *Friedrich Hölderlin: Poems and Fragments*, 4th edn (London: Anvil, 2004), 551.]

V.

Afterword

The fascination issuing from Schelling's metaphysics is due to the circumstance that his excavating thought reaches strata in which beings are no longer rooted, but all roots decompose: it reaches an abyss for reason which is nevertheless also its presupposition since it must precisely keep its distance from it. From this conception, there shines a modernity we have not yet reached. Schelling, namely, keeps equally much distance from the naïve optimism of rationalist reason and from the escapist pessimism of relativist reason. He offers instead the theory of a rationality that has the property of being necessarily, rather than contingently, endangered. Without this danger it would lose the energy of its self-maintenance, but it must at the same time keep this energy source at a distance. What gives reason its force is not its home, but rather a presupposition to be recollected and avoided at the same time. Rationality, in essence, is at risk of losing both its distance from the origin and its contact with it. The modernity of this perspective is this: we may henceforth call a behaviour rational that remains just as aware of its presuppositions and that cannot be recouped directly from them. Both are required: the ascertaining of that history in which we stand, as well as the distance from its binding force. This cross takes upon itself, and positively, the risk of losing its balance. The positivity of this risk is the index of the historicity of rationality that is not to be removed: it is merely the successful, that is, vulnerable outcome of an antagonism, not itself temporal [*zeitlich*] but productive [*zeitigenden*], between inconsistent energy and the demand for consistency.

Taken universally, this syndrome is, according to Schelling, compatible with a cosmological interpretation: henceforth the rationality of *homo sapiens* is only the echo of a cosmogonic process that, in the manner of an auto-epistemic universe, remains operative in our cognitive constitution. *After Schelling, epistemology is thus cosmology in one*, always presupposing that there is only one universe. This monistic thesis can only be sustained if it happens that, in the emergence of the universe, there is already that being operative that hereafter steps forth as mind. Only if this methodological trick can be justified does the thesis of the identity of epistemology and cosmology hold. And only once this is secured is there a metaphysics in a sense worthy of the name. The metaphysical project is not in conflict with the sciences, but with myth. In this sense, Schelling's *The Ages of the World* still remains oriented towards carrying out the earliest system-programme of German idealism, with its demand for a new mythology, a mythology of reason.

What may today still seem something we can get a handle on in this project is of course the predication-theoretical element of his metaphysics, by which our reconstruction has let itself be guided. Doubtless not all of Schelling's intentions are caught through this lens, but perhaps at least this, that his project can be considered as a prelude to a metaphysics that has not yet been written. In the meantime, it is not to be understood as one that is interpreted as a theory of epistemic maxima, that could or would like to vie with the sciences for certainty, but rather as a theory of epistemic minima, stationed in the risk-filled domain of rationality, for 'spirit only occupies itself with objects so long as there is something secret, not revealed in them'.[1] In this minimal sense, metaphysics is in fact a science of the secret, not one that would have to shun the light of day, but one that is indeed at home, if we are not persuaded of it, where we always are: lost in thought.

The design of such a metaphysics as fundamental heuristics evidently breaks with Kant from the legacy of rational theology, but continues further along his regulative 'way out' of the metaphysical resource of phenomena, in order to ground it more deeply with Schelling. For Kant forgot to pose the question what it means for subjectivity as a worldly being to be oriented towards a regulatively characterised horizon. As noted, this orientation was anchored by Plato in the structure of an *apomantic soul*[2] that precedes *apophantic logos*. With Aristotle, this orientation can also be designated a natural *epistemic orexia*.[3] This can be added to. For in returning to the intentional vector, which our identifying and predicating articulations of the world only ever actualise, metaphysics acquires a modest form as the theory of our orientation towards something. In this way, it breaks with its traditional role as nominal metaphysics and acquires the contours of a pronominal metaphysics. For the stated orientation can fit well into a pre-predicative search model, that is simply pronominally informed. This search model establishes the ongoing nominal search that, for the meaning of Something whatever that exists, has always already been pronominally discoverable: *knowledge by acquaintance of boundless existence*.[4]

And if we group that discovery as a feedback effect,[5] then what we otherwise call consciousness comes to be recognised as the feedback of this pronominal discovery. This is all the more clear the more distinctly the orientation towards anything whatever comes to the fore, and is nevertheless as a rule considered nominal. Pronominal orientation also ensures that we are *a priori* beyond all limits, nominally transfinite, and these limits and definitions can therefore be recognised as limit-definitions in general, that is, limitative competences.

In this sense the transfinite search model guarantees precisely that our information processing remains open. But what does this mean? Is this openness itself another property of neuroanatomical equipment? We would then have to take into account a system that is itself materially active and works receptively; but it is this, however, precisely only by orientation towards an immaterial, completely indeterminate pole. If this orientation itself is another product of the neuronal mechanism, then our information processing operates under its own resources. Its finite operations are possible in consequence of its transfinite prologue. If this is the case, then to be consistent, we must say that our brain has itself created a window, out of which of course we do not lean, nor indeed can we see out of it, but that certainly lets in the opalescent shimmering of indeterminacy. This pale light generates a heliotropism, that is, a monotropism for information processing and, to this end, there is the transfinite search model, which alone makes epistemic finitism possible. It is not therefore the determinacy that is the real puzzle, the nominal yield of our epistemic efforts, but rather the indeterminacy, the nerve of metaphysics or, in Schellingian style, the original negation. Against this, semantic idealism shatters. The true is then the whole except for One.

Notes

1. G. W. F. Hegel, *Aesthetics* [trans. T. M. Knox (Oxford: Oxford University Press, 1975), 604].
2. Cf. Plato, *Republic* 505e: 'Ψυχή ... ἀπομαντευομένη τί εἶναι'.
3. Cf. Aristotle, *Metaphysics* [trans. H. Treddenick (Cambridge, MA: Harvard University Press, 1968)], 980a22: 'Πάντες ἄνθρωποι του ειδεναι τι ὀρέγονται φυσει [All men naturally desire knowledge]'.
4. [In English in the original.]
5. Cf. Karl Duncker, *Zur Psychologie des produktiven Denkens* (1935) (Berlin: Springer, 1966), 90.

Postface
The Ontology of Predication in Schelling's *The Ages of the World*

Markus Gabriel

Since the introduction to the *Freedom* essay at the latest, the problem of identity shifted to the centre of Schelling's thinking. By the 'problem of identity', I understand the question as to how an identity claim can be both informative and non-contradictory. At first sight A = B appears to mean either that A is not really B but just A, or we are dealing with a contradiction. 'A' and 'B' either refer to the same (that is, to A or indeed to B) or they really refer to A and B, but then the claim is false, that is, contradictory. As Wittgenstein writes in the *Tractatus logico-philosophicus*, 'Casually speaking: to say of *two* things that they are identical is meaningless, and to say of *one* that it is identical to itself says nothing at all.'[1] Wittgenstein concludes from this that no essential metaphysical (for him: logical) function can be ascribed to identity expressed through the equals sign. We either share the basic assumptions behind this or we do not. It is clear that for Schelling, it is insufficient to formulate the problem of identity in order to erase it, in general keeping with Wittgenstein's method. In a way, Schelling instead begins where Wittgenstein leaves off.

Even in his identity-philosophy phase, Schelling already suspects that the problem of identity exists, though it is only in the middle period of his philosophy that he begins to address the problem. In the background lies an interesting identity theory of judgement. A standard objection to the identity theory runs that the copula 'is' in 'A is B' cannot designate identity. If I say 'Peter is large', I am not of course saying that Peter is identical with being large. This is precisely what Schelling does not maintain, pointing out instead that identity does not have to mean 'one-and-the-same' or oneness.[2] 'Oneness' here means *strict identity*, which obtains just when A and B have the same properties in every respect and at every level: $\forall x \forall y[x = y \Rightarrow \forall E(Ex \Leftrightarrow Ey)]$, where 'E' here, as noted, includes every respect and every level. In the strict sense of identity 2 + 2 could not = 4 since 2 + 2 have properties other than does 4, such as being divided into two equally large natural numbers that are combined by addition, which does not apply to the single number. For this reason, strict identity can only obtain where no information results, that is by manifest tautologies such as

(T) The one horse called Ulrich is identical with the one horse called Ulrich

Among the circumstances that (T) assumes are that there is such a horse, which we can dispute. In any case, we cannot only make self-evident tautologies, since then we would also have to accept

(T²) The round square is a round square.

(T²) cannot be true, since round squares cannot exist. But once the apparent constraint that there is such a horse is fulfilled, (T) concerns a case of oneness. Nor can this be what is intended in ontology. When we propose some identity theory of body and soul (or in more contemporary terms, of brain and mind), we necessarily maintain that brain and mind are one in precisely that way as the singular horse called Ulrich is self-identical. This is in any case what the eliminative materialists maintain, and they thereby still owe us an explanation as to why we use different terms, such as 'brain' and 'mind', and different languages to make sense of the two terms.

Schelling presents his analysis of informative and non-contradictory judgements of identity particularly clearly in the following passage from *The Ages of the World*. He argues there that while

> one cannot come right out and say that the soul is the body or the body is the soul, it is certainly legitimate to observe that that which in

one regard is the body is in another regard the soul [...] The proper meaning, for example, of the simple judgment that A is B is actually this: *the something that is A is the something that is also B.* In this manner, one can clearly see that the copula lies at the basis not only of the predicates, but also of the subject. What is at stake here is not a simple unity, but rather a unity that has been doubled, an identity of identity. In the proposition A is B, three propositions are implicit: first, the proposition A is X (X is the not always explicitly named 'one and the same thing,' of which the subject and the predicate are both predicates); second, the proposition X is B. Only thereby that the two judgments are bound together again, that is, through the reduplication of the copula, does the third proposition A is B emerge.[3]

If, as an example, we take the judgement,

(J) Peter is large,

Schelling's analysis of the judgement states that there is an X that in one respect is Peter and in another respect is large. This X can be presented pronominally as what Wolfram Hogrebe calls 'pronominal being' in his trailblazing reconstruction of Schelling's theory of predication.[4] The judgement (J) refers to something about which it judges both that it is Peter and that it is large.

Among other things, we note that it is possible that the judgement may turn out to be false in both respects. (J) is equally false when this is not Peter (but Andreas) as when it is indeed Peter, but he is not large. A third presupposition of (J) that we will discuss is that there is something in general, that there is an X that we individuate as being both Peter and as being large. Hence the following analysis of (J):

(J*) ∃x (Px & Lx)

According to Schelling's analysis, (J) therefore consists in at least two truth-apt judgements, namely Px and Gx, which he calls the '*Reduplikation des Bandes*', the 'reduplication' or 'doubling of the copula'.[5] The reason for this is easily understood: in the judgement 'Peter is large' we had just one copula, albeit one that internally divides into

(J2) 'X is P'

and

(J3) 'X is L'

As a result, however, a fatal problem seems already to arise. If the analysis of (J) led to a reduplication, doesn't this entail an analysis of (U2) and (U3) as necessitating additional reduplication? We would then have to accept

(J2*) ∃y (Xy & Py)

as an intermediary step. We can call this the problem of the 'regress of judgement'. In order that this does not set up a fatal regress, we must look out for a well-founded regress stopper in Schelling. My thesis is that Schelling does in fact introduce a regress stopper that he calls 'indifference'. The other names he uses for this are 'indifference point' and, following the *Freedom* essay, 'unground'.[6] Before discussing an interesting passage in this regard, I would like to sketch the train of thought informing this.

Take (J) once more. In the analysis, it was shown that there is something that is both Peter and that is large. This is particularly evident if we understand that (J) can be false in at least two ways. If the large person there is not Peter, she may still be large. The false judgement was partly false. It follows from this that 'Peter' does not function pronominally, that is, that Peter is not a logically proper name but is tied to a description. Peter is, as it were, 'the person I have known for many years' or 'Johanna's friend'. 'Peter' does not mean 'that person there'. We do not directly pick Peter out. But what then do we pick out directly? Schelling's answer is that we just have to acknowledge that there is something that, whatever it is, we pick out when we judge it to be large. (J) would also then be true if we only hallucinate largeness there. Even a hallucinated colour patch would appear large, for instance, if it appeared to us as large as Peter. In a certain sense, it would still be legitimate to say that this-there (the hallucinated colour patch) is perhaps unusually large for an afterimage. The 'X' in the analysis of (J) is therefore a placeholder, standing for 'whatever it is that I am referring to'; it is a universal logically proper name that is precisely objectively defined in every instance, which is why we can be mistaken about it.

But what exactly is the presumed categorial difference between the judgement 'this-there is Peter' and the judgement 'Peter is large'? The contrast Schelling envisions becomes apparent when we realise that we cannot ask whether 'this-there' really is 'this-there', although we can ask whether 'this-there' is in fact Peter. 'This-there' is a logically proper name with the specific property of being universal, since everything can become a 'this-there' whenever we pass a judgement. Universal, pronominal being is only individuated when, in normal judgements, we refer to Something whatever and recognise that this capacity presupposes that we are referring to Something whatever that, whatever it might be, 'is'. This Something whatever is indifferent in relation to the descriptions we have to use in order to make it cognisable or to individuate it epistemically. The regress of judgements breaks off by way of the introduction of logically proper names, and indeed a universal logically proper name. (J2) properly reads

(J2**) This-there is Peter

From which we cannot in turn infer that

(J2***) There is a This-there such that This-there is a This-there: $\exists Tt\ (TtTt)$

In (J2***) we are dealing with an expression of indifference, that is, no further information is provided. (J2***) thus violates a criterion for our speaking of judgement, in respect of which we can still distinguish between subject and predicate. '[T]here are no judgments that assert simple sameness, neither in a repetitive proposition nor in its explanation. Without first understanding a twofold, the assertion of unity has no meaning.'[7]

When we assert of This-there simply that there is a This-there, and no further information as to This-there is available, we have reached the position of 'equal validity' or indifference:[8] anything whatever is a 'This-there'. Unlike Russell's logical atomism, Schelling does not conclude from this that we must assume a fundamental referential stratum with which we are familiar, and which Russell designated 'knowledge by acquaintance'.[9] From the outset, Schelling avoids the assumption of anything corresponding to 'protocol sentences' which register only that there is a This-there, since he acknowledges that we are not, at this level, dealing with judgement proper.

At this point I would like to discuss two objections that will illuminate matters. The first objection says that there are many properties that all beings have in common: the property of being identical to itself; the property of being something that has properties; the property of becoming describable only if certain logical laws or rules are accepted, etc. We may call these properties *metaphysical* or *logical properties*.[10] Being-a-This-there seems to be just one among many such metaphysical or logical properties, that is, a property that applies to everything that is at all. Traditionally, logical-metaphysical properties could also be designated using the shorthand 'ontological properties'.[11] This being the case, Schelling's decision to halt the judgement regress by means of the property of being-a-This-there would be arbitrary: we could choose any ontological property from however many and obtain different results.

This objection, however, overlooks the fact that the property of being-a-This-there is a property that applies to all objects individuatingly, which is what I am getting at with the concept of universal logical proper names. This-there is already individuated by what we articulate in the judgement. When I judge that This-there is Peter and that Peter is large, this 'This-there' is no anonymous something-or-other.[12] It is exactly 'This-there' that in one respect is Peter and in another is large. This corresponds generally to Aristotle's distinction between prime matter (πρώτη ὕλη) and this-there (τόδε τι). Whereas prime matter is without properties and unstructured, each This-there is already individuated, which is why we can address them in judgements about This-there. We cannot say anything about prime matter, but we can about This-there. Schelling does not halt the judgement regress by introducing an object undifferentiated in itself, perhaps 'the Absolute', as Hegel famously objected against him in the Preface to the *Phenomenology of Spirit*.[13] In analysing the judgement, we instead discover that we refer to a differentiated actuality consisting in individuals, and so we conceptually integrate these individuals by way of our judgement practices, wherein we take them as universal logically proper names, that is, as This-there. I see this consideration lying behind the following, crucial passage, which I quote at length and would like to introduce into the discussion:

> It is a different mode of unity [*Einheit* as opposed to *Einerleiheit*, M.G.] that emerges simultaneously with the antithesis, insofar as the will of contraction makes itself into the bond [= copula, M.G.] of subject and object. In this way, as the unifying middle, it steps forth as the first active agent [*das erste Wirkende*], representing what is common to both wills and has grown out of them. In relationship to what holds them together, the two competing wills are completely equal forms of existence. While existentially equal, they are of course essentially unequal, and relate themselves as higher and lower. When we have spoken of the equal-validity (*die Gleich-Gültigkeit*) or the indifference of both, we have had this existential equality in mind, that is, the equality of both principles in relationship to the real existent.[14]

The regress stopper appears as such from the moment we identify the regress. As Schelling writes, it is for this reason that it 'emerges simultaneously with the antithesis'. But this means that we do not have to assume that there is some in itself undifferentiated matter, a singular This-there that, as it were, we split by judging and transform into individuals. This process remains completely incomprehensible, which is why, in *The Ages of the World*, Schelling distances himself from the thought of emanation from a unity or from a fall from the absolute.[15]

One can also take a less speculative approach to this thought process, in the following way. Gottlob Frege suggested a useful context principle: 'Only in the context of a proposition do words refer to something.'[16] This means that neither 'Peter' nor 'is large' are meaningful in themselves independently of being integrated into a proposition. There are, accordingly, no semantic atoms that are meaningful independently of being articulated in a judgement. We can, however, analyse judgements, as Schelling himself undertakes when he formulates the 'basic laws governing judgments'.[17] In the analysis of judgements we recognise the reduplication and thus encounter indifference as a necessary regress stopper. We are therefore justified in assuming that there is not just one, single This-there, but that 'This-there' is precisely a universal logical proper name. Through the analysis of judgements, we recognise that there is a reality differentiated in itself to which we refer, even when we are often mistaken in determining the exact constituents of this reality.

The second objection states that the criteria Schelling uses to define the concept of judgement are arbitrary. For example, he expressly says that we are only judging when we use at least two concepts.[18] It is precisely this assumption that allows him to halt the regress because he can in this way distinguish between indifference (one-and-the-same-ness) and unity. Nevertheless, Schelling certainly has other arguments available here. Specifically, he can point out that he is speaking about judgements rather than propositions or facts. In a judgement, we put forward a thought as true. We affirm that such and such is the case or that the thought 'T' is true. Suchlike assertions have little meaning when we affirm that A = A or that A is A. For even when we might characterise an assertion as *true* or even as logically true, this is not a meaningful *assertion*. For we only assert that a thought is true if this is contested or contestable. In Wittgenstein we read, again with a slightly different thrust:

> The identity of the meaning of two expressions cannot be asserted. For in order to be able to assert anything about their meaning, I must know their meaning, and if I know their meaning, I know whether they mean the same or something different.[19]

Like Hölderlin and Hegel, Schelling hears 'part' (*Teil*) expressed in the word 'judgement' (*Urteil*). Judgement is the partition of a prior unity. We formulate this prior unity as sameness and thus discover the regress stopper. By our practice of judging, however, we know that the regress stopper must be differentiated in itself. It fulfils the same function every time, but the This-there is every time replaceable by another.

Schelling also articulates this thought with the assertion

> that every being that is (*ein jedes Seyende*) should, at the same time, be something that is both being and nonbeing, in that being (*das Seyn*) is precisely that in it, which is not a being that is.[20]

Wolfram Hogrebe has introduced the concept of a 'dimension of distinction', that is, a dimension that we differentiate as such when we encounter distinctions.[21] 'Being' (*das Seyn*) here seems to me to correspond exactly to such a dimension of distinction. Assume that we had a simplified dimension of distinction made up of just the concept 'being-red'. We differentiate it when we say that the table is red. The table thereby appears in the dimension of distinction. It is something that is red (*ein Rot-Seiendes*). This does not, however, mean that by this means, being-red has somehow become something that is red. Being-red cannot itself appear as something red in a dimension of distinction made up of red.

We can also understand 'being (*das Seyn*)' with the help of the following thought-experiment. Let us assume that we live in a world in which all objects are red. In this case, the assertion that an object is red does not distinguish it from other objects. Now assume another world, a green world, in which all objects are green. We can imagine innumerable worlds in which there is exactly one property shared by all objects that appear in it, such that this very property cannot informatively be attributed to it. For in a world in which everything is red, we gain no information about any object by learning only that it is red. 'Being (*das Seyn*)' is the universal idea of a property that happens to apply to everything, that is, the universal idea of the dimension of distinction, independently of the question of precisely what property it might be in a world. 'Being' is therefore never something that is, although it is internally differentiated in everything that is. Schelling himself writes that 'being' is internally differentiated.

> There is ... [in] being (*das Seyn*) a back-and-forth between scission and union. Or, more precisely stated, it is the division within ... being that conditions the primary division between being and what is being. Both divisions collapse into one.[22]

There are good reasons for this assumption. The most important is that we could not explain how judgement comes about at all if we started from an undifferentiated being. We cannot transform an in-itself undifferentiated reality of the *apeiron* type into differentiated relations.

Let us again return to solving the problem of identity. As we said, this problem consists in the question of how identity claims can be at the same time informative and non-contradictory. This is not possible for strict identity. Hence Schelling distinguishes between sameness and unity. Let us now take up Frege's basic idea, which partly illuminates our problematic. Frege resolves the problem of identity by introducing the concept of sense in 'On Sense and Reference'.[23] As is well known, he asserts that there is always something in an identity claim to which two terms differently refer. In consequence, there is always a difference in meaning, in the types of givenness, in identity of reference. The expressions 'The Evening star is the Morning star' and 'Evening star = Morning star' mean that there is something (namely, the planet Venus) that appears in one way in the morning and in another in the evening. The same thing appears in two distinct ways. The differentiation of perspectives allows Frege to resolve the problem of identity. Indeed, he repeats Schelling's position that there is an X that is equally the Morning as the Evening star.

The difference seems to lie in the fact that Frege identifies this X when he addresses it as 'Venus'. On its own, of course, this doesn't work. For, as Frege himself acknowledges, the proper name 'Venus' has itself a sense, presenting the star as what grounds, so to speak, its appearance as both Evening star and Morning star. This starts the regress. Frege's thought continues here when, like Schelling, he introduces a universal reference, that is, a reference variable that cannot be exhausted by any description or sense, such that the assertion '"Venus" is what grounds' is already in fact an illegitimate oversimplification.

> The sense of a proper name is grasped by everybody who is sufficiently familiar with the language or totality of designations to which it belongs; but this serves to illuminate the *Bedeutung*, supposing it present, only one-sidedly. Comprehensive knowledge of the *Bedeutung* would require us to be able to say immediately whether any given sense attaches to it. To such knowledge we never attain.[24]

Unfortunately, Frege solves the problem only pragmatically by assuming that a *Bedeutung*, that is, something to which we refer, is already available: 'we presuppose a *Bedeutung*'.[25] Frege himself formulates the objection that we could be wrong about this. Sometimes we hold something to exist independently of our representing it which in fact does not. In his view, in such cases would still have a sense, but no reference.

Now we can, of course, be mistaken in the presupposition, and such mistakes have indeed occurred. But the question whether the presupposition is perhaps always mistaken need not be answered here; in order to justify speaking of the *Bedeutung* of a sign, it is enough, at first, to point out our intention in speaking or thinking. (We must then add the reservation: provided such a *Bedeutung* exists.)[26]

Schelling, by contrast, is not satisfied with a pragmatic solution. For he recognises that we cannot rely on a singular block referent, a maximal object, whose existence we presuppose. Rather, we must make further assumptions regarding the identity of that whose existence we affirm. We can almost reconstruct *The Ages of the World* as an attempt to discover the minimal conditions for our presupposing that we sometimes refer to something that, sufficiently individuated, already exists prior to the reference. Schelling is concerned to think individuation independently of conceptual or propositional individuation. We do not impose the conditions of individuation in conceptual or propositional form on a reality unarticulated in itself. Yet this means that neither can we rely on a being correlated to every difference. The dimension of distinction cannot be thought of in so standardised a manner. Or Schelling once more:

> There is ... [in] being (*das Seyn*) a back-and-forth between scission and union. Or, more precisely stated, it is the division within ... being that conditions the primary division between being and what is being. Both divisions collapse into one.[27]

I understand this statement as follows. When we judge of something as being such-and-such, it emerges against a background of possibilities and actualities. We have selected something and combined it with possible predicates. Now we might believe that the domain from which we select is in itself predicatively undifferentiated. One argument for this could be derived from the fact that our predications rely on a distinction between (saturated) objects and their properties (expressed by unsaturated functions), while reality can hardly consist of free-floating objects on the one hand and free-floating properties on the other. Reality is predicatively saturated. Reality must accordingly be predicatively undifferentiated. Yet this overlooks Schelling's principal insight: *every statement about reality takes place in reality since one can say something about the statement.* If we can abstract from the saturation in our judgements in order to extract the property-function '... is a P', this procedure again takes place in reality.

I have elsewhere called this basic idea, variants of which are also found in Hegel and Fichte, 'transcendental ontology'.[28] By this

I mean any ontology that takes into account that judgements, opinions, convictions, propositions and so on must always belong to the reality to which they refer. For that reason, we can be exactly as mistaken about judgements as about other objects, precisely because we refer to them fallibly. The predicative divide, the 'primordial partition' or *judgement* (*die Ur-teil*), takes place in the midst of being, such that the dualism of a monistic being on the one hand and the plurality of discursive practices on the other is *a limine* overcome. Schelling therefore does not once set foot in the territory of the Cartesian assumption that there is on the one hand mindless extension (*res extensa* = world) and on the other a fallible mind (*res cogitans*). Mind and world cannot meaningfully be distinguished such that two completely distinct domains are assigned to them. Schelling manifestly takes this idea from Spinoza. He also accepts, however, that we ought therefore to assume that our judgements take place in the midst of a reality that does not lie behind the judgements. When I judge that Friedrich judges it to be raining, we do not for one moment find a real event behind the fact that Friedrich judges and that is distinct from Friedrich's judgements.

To conclude, I would like to discuss another quite radical innovation of Schelling's, which removes him from classical Western metaphysics. One articulation of this innovation is the following proposition: 'Priority stands in inverse relationship to superiority.'[29] Classical Western metaphysics had until Schelling assumed that what is first in the metaphysical order is also the good, since the first was introduced as the *archē* by which everything else might even be. If anything at all exists, it must be the principle of order that is in consequence the foundation of existence. Schelling, however, clearly sees that not everything pre-existent can be called 'good' just because it exists or is something at all. He concludes from this that in the best case, the foundation of existence is neutral in respect of value. Hogrebe gets to the point when he writes:

> Like no other, Nietzsche included, Schelling investigated the inner possibility of the suspicion of meaninglessness, with the result that there is absolutely no sense that is above such 'suspicion' provided that the question of what it means that something exists is sufficiently radically posed. For the original ground of meaninglessness is precisely existence itself. That is: what in the end we

understand being to be is something antecedent to all meaning. In this insight the *secret of the world* is finally revealed to Schelling: *being is senseless*.[30]

Since the *Freedom* essay, then, Schelling distinguished between the unground (the first) and love. Love is what transcends potentially meaningless being. It is his name for successful relationships. In the predicative domain love would be a true judgement that surprisingly refers to something whose identity we had not previously established. Love is the bond, as Schelling, following Plato, repeatedly says; it is what successfully suspends the regress in a true judgement.

> Existence is separation, the singularity of what is one's *own* (*Eigenheit*). Love, however, is the nothing of ownness, it does not look out for its own and cannot therefore ever be existent on its own.[31]

The concept of love introduces a third dimension to the theory of predication. The first dimension is indifference, that is, the dimension of the universal, logical proper name of 'This-there'. Corresponding to this dimension is the presupposition of an of itself pre-individuated dimension of distinction to which we refer in judgements. The second dimension is the judgements themselves, which only cover part of the first dimension, since we are very far from having predicatively articulated reality as a whole. These two dimensions are forms of 'sorting', in that on the one hand they consist in individuals and on the other in the individual variables we explicitly individuate and hence describe in judgements. Nor do we have the slightest grasp of how the first and second dimensions cohere; the most prominent candidate among them for this coherence would be truth. Schelling himself speaks here in one breath of 'spirit' and 'love'.[32] In my reconstruction, the issue here is synonyms for the thought of a universality that is more than the sum of all logical proper names, that is, a connection that does not arise only through abstraction. 'Spirit' and 'love' indicate that the world exhibits a genuine structure of facts that we express in true judgements. The traditional name for this was 'intelligibility'. Beings were ascribed intelligibility on the basis of ascribing to them an ordering principle that Schelling rejects, because he does not start from intelligibility but from being, which is not yet sense.

Viewed against this background, Schelling also influenced thinkers of hope, Ernst Bloch above all, because he offered a form of thought that did not already assume that the world was good, beautiful and true, but aimed instead to produce intelligibility by actions and judgements. Schelling sees particularly clearly that order is fragile and contingent, which is incompatible with the ancient idea that the world is embedded in necessity, in *anankē*. Schelling distributes the functions corresponding to the *archē* over three dimensions, whereby he understands these three dimensions as the genuine dimension of time.

Notes

1. Wittgenstein, *TLP* 5.5303.
2. Schelling also distinguishes between 'oneness' and 'unity'. See, for instance, SW I/8, 213 [*Ages*, 8].
3. *Weltalter*, 28 [*Ages 1811*, 87].
4. See in particular § 17 of *Predication and Genesis*, pp. 92–7 above.
5. [*Ages 1811*, 87].
6. On the concept and function of the 'unground', see especially Markus Gabriel, *Das Absolute und die Welt in Schellings Freiheitsschrift* [*The Absolute and the World in Schelling's Freedom Essay*] (Bonn: Bonn University Press, 2006), and 'Der Ungrund als das uneinholbar Andere der Reflexion: Schellings Ausweg aus dem Idealismus' ['The Unground as the Insuperable Other of Reflection: Schelling's Way Out of Idealism'], in D. Ferre and T. Pedro (eds), *Schellings Philosophie der Freiheit: Studien zu den Philosophischen Untersuchungen über das Wesen der Menschlichen Freiheit*, Studien Zur Phanomenologie und Praktischen Philosophie, 28 (Würzburg: Ergon, 2012), 177–90.
7. *Weltalter*, 27 [*Ages 1811*, 85]. Compare I/8, 213 [*Ages*, 8: 'because in no judgment whatsoever, not even in the merely tautological, is it expressed that [what is] combined (the subject and the predicate) are one and the same. Rather, there is only an identity of the being [*Einheit des Wesens*], of the link (the copula) – tr.].
8. *Weltalter*, 26: 'Gleich-Gültigkeit' [*Ages 1811*, 85].
9. See Bertrand Russell's classic essay, 'Knowledge by Acquaintance and Knowledge by Description', *Proceedings of the Aristotelian Society* (New Series), vol. 11 (1910–11), 108–28.
10. On this, see Colin McGinn, *Logical Properties: Identity, Existence, Predication, Necessary Truth* (Oxford: Oxford University Press, 2000).
11. For various reasons I reject this identification. On this, see especially Markus Gabriel, *Fields of Sense: A New Realist Ontology* (Edinburgh: Edinburgh University Press, 2014).
12. On the anonymous something-or-other, which he calls '*n'importe quoi*', see Tristan Garcia, *Forme et objet: un traité des choses* (Paris: PUF, 2010) [*Form and Object. A Treatise on Things*, trans. Mark Allan Ohm and Jon Cogburn (Edinburgh: Edinburgh University Press, 2014].

13. See the well-known passage in the 'Preface' to the *Phenomenology of Spirit*, where Hegel, discussing 'A = A', writes: 'To pit this single insight [*dies Eine Wissen*], that in the Absolute everything is the same, against the full body of articulated cognition, which at least seeks and demands such fulfilment, to palm off its Absolute as the night in which all cows are black – this is cognition naïvely reduced to vacuity' [trans. A. V. Miller (Oxford: Oxford University Press, 1977), 9].
14. *Weltalter*, 26 [*Ages 1811*, 85].
15. Compare, for instance, from *Weltalter*, 17 [*Ages 1811*, 74]: 'But what might have moved beatific bliss (*Seligkeit*) to abandon its lucid purity and step out into being? – This is what one usually finds puzzling in the question of the relationship of eternity to being, of the infinite to the finite. As has been often enough noted, it would be impossible for such lucid purity to step out of itself, impossible for it to discharge or cast something out of itself, or for it in any way to act upon an outside. Even that might be saying too much, for how could anything at all unfold in it? It is entirely one with its deed and is itself that deed.'
16. Gottlob Frege, *Foundations of Arithmetic. A Logico-mathematical Enquiry into the Concept of Number*, trans. Dale Jacquette (Abingdon: Routledge, 2016), 66. Compare Wittgenstein's variant, the detail of which has very different implications, in *TLP* 3.3: 'Only the proposition has sense; only in the context of a proposition has a name meaning.'
17. *Weltalter*, 27: 'der ersten Gesetze jedes Urtheils' [*Ages 1811*, 85].
18. Cf. *Weltalter*, 27 [*Ages 1811*, 85: 'without always first understanding a twofold, the assertion of unity has no meaning' – tr.].
19. Wittgenstein, *TLP* 6.2322.
20. *Weltalter*, 27 [*Ages 1811*, 86].
21. Wolfram Hogrebe, *Echo des Nichtwissens* [*Echo of Unknowing*] (Berlin: Akademie, 2006), 317: 'Every introduction of basic differences exploits this distinction dimension. It cannot be further differentiated from other spaces, indeed cannot be positively characterised at all, and yet we need it because otherwise we could not generate a universe by our distinctions. Semantically, it is the completely diaphanous background of every semantic contrast, the transcendental condition of their possibility.' On this, see also my contribution to Hogrebe's *Festschrift*, 'Die Welt als konstitutiver Entzug' ['The World as Constitutive Withdrawal'], which also draws on Hogrebe's work, in Guido Kreis and Joachim Bromand (eds), *Was sich nicht sagen lässt: Das Nicht-Begriffliche in Wissenschaft, Kunst und Religion* [*What Cannot be Said: The Non-Conceptual in Science, Art and Religion*] (Berlin: Akademie, 2010), 85–100. On Hogrebe's philosophy, see also my 'On Wolfram Hogrebe's Approach to Philosophy', in Markus Gabriel and Jens Halfwassen (eds), *Gadamerprofessur 2006: Wolfram Hogrebe: 'Die Wirklichkeit des Denkens* [*Wolfram Hogrebe, Gadamer Professor 2006: 'The Actuality of Thought'*] (Heidelberg: Winter, 2007), 84–104.
22. *Weltalter*, 36 [*Ages 1811*, 95].
23. See Frege, 'On *Sinn* and *Bedeutung*', in Michael Beaney (ed.), *The Frege Reader* (Oxford: Blackwell, 1997), 151–71.
24. Ibid., 153, translation modified.
25. Ibid., 156.
26. Ibid., 156.

27. *Weltalter*, 36 [*Ages 1811*, 95].
28. See Markus Gabriel, *Transcendental Ontology: Essays in German Idealism* (London: Continuum, 2011).
29. *Weltalter*, 26 [*Ages 1811*, 85].
30. Hogrebe, *Prädikation und Genesis*, 13 [p. 8, in translation above].
31. *Weltalter*, 19 [*Ages 1811*, 77].
32. On the predication-theoretical reconstruction of the concept of spirit, see Hogrebe's remark in *Prädikation und Genesis*, 102 [p. 96, in translation above], where he introduces 'propositional variables or the propositional dimension', which can be distinguished from the dimension of distinction, or being.

Index

a priori self-enlarging judgement *see* synthetic *a priori*
Adorno, T., 106
aesthetic idealism, 15–16, 19
aesthetics, 12, 106
affirmation *see Ages of the World, The* (Schelling): original negation and original affirmation
Ages of the World, The (Schelling)
  approach to, 6–8
  argumentative reconstruction, 28–9
  as biography, xxiv–xxvi
  from chaos to order, 92–7
  Dante as archetype for, 24–8
  identity theory of judgement, 127–8
  new mythology, 23–4
  original negation and original affirmation, 77–87
  predication theory, 75–7
  predicative rotation, 87–92
  reason and madness, 109–17
  self-organisation and unity, 97–102
  world formula, 103–8
algorithms, 51
analytic idealism, 5
analytic philosophy of language, 37, 43, 44

Aristotle, 6, 58, 62, 124, 131
art *see Philosophy of Art* (Schelling)
art-object, 106
Art of Life, The (Schelling), 22
Auerbach, E., 13
auto-epistemic structure of world / universe, x, xx, 46–8, 49, 51, 73, 107, 123

Baudelaire, C., xxix
becoming, 86–7, 87–8, 91–2
beginning *see* genesis of the universe
beginning potentials, theory of, 82–7
beginning variables, 93–5
beginnings, proposition concerning the conservation of knowledge of, 73–4
being, xv–xvi
  dimension of distinction, 133–4, 136
  meaning of, xv, xvi, 8, 112–13
  meaninglessness of, xii–xiii, 8, 62
  predicative, 63, 64, 65: from chaos to order, 93, 95; original negation and original affirmation, 78, 79, 80–1, 82, 84–5; self-organisation, 99, 100
  primordial, 79, 80

pronominal, xi, 63–4, 65, 67, 128, 130: from chaos to order, 93, 95, 96; original negation and original affirmation, 78–9, 80–1, 82, 84, 85; self-organisation, 99, 100; world formula, 105
propositional, 65, 67, 82, 94, 95, 99
see also Dasein
Berlin Academy of Sciences, 28–9, 36, 69, 76
Blanchot, M., xi
Bloch, E., 139
Böhme, J., 26
Bredekamp, H., xxxii

Cartesian theory, 114–15, 137
consciousness, 73, 79, 97, 105, 110–11, 114–15, 124; *see also* Mitwissenschaft; self-consciousness
construction, xv–xvi; *see also* self-construction
constructivism, xx
continuation potential, 82, 84–5
continuous determination, principle of, 53
cosmic inconsistency, 89–90, 107, 108
cosmology, 60–1
Critique of Pure Reason (*CPR*, Kant), xii, 53

Dante, 11–14, 19–21, 24–8
Dasein, 115; *see also* being
descriptive metaphysics, 42
determinability, principle of, 53
dimension of distinction, 133–4, 136
Dionysus, 109–10
discourse-analytic potential of philosophy, 5–6
discourse-creating potential of philosophy, 6
discrete ontology, 41, 43, 55
distinctions / discrimination, 38–9, 40

Divina Commedia (Dante), 11–12, 13–14, 19–21, 33n53
as archetype for *The Ages of the World*, 24–8
dualism, xxvi, 50, 51–2, 80, 96, 137; *see also* Cartesian theory

Enlightenment thesis, 15–16
enslaving principle, 98
epistemic communism, 15
epistemology, xiv, 18, 123
participant epistemology, xv
see also auto-epistemic structure of world / universe; knowledge
equal validity, 130
Erlangen Lectures (Schelling), 22, 24
essence, 44–5
soul-like, 99
events, 66
existence *see* being

Fa-judgements, 37, 40–1, 43, 49, 63, 70n14, 75–6
facts, 66
Fichte, J.G., xxx–xxxi, xxxii, 13, 18
freedom, 16, 20, 94, 100, 102, 108
Frege, G., 57, 101–2, 103, 132, 134–5
Friedrich, W.P., 13
Fuchs, C.-C., 14

genesis of the universe, 60–2, 63, 107–8; *see also* beginnings, proposition concerning the conservation of knowledge of
God, xxiv, xxvi, 26, 28, 113
Goethe, J.W.v., xxxi–xxxii, 12
Goodman, N., 40–1
'Greek Sphinx with Nemesis' Wheel', 1

Haken, H., 98–9, 119n74
Hasenjaeger, G., 41, 54
Heavenly Image, The (Schlegel), 11
Hegel, G.W.F., xxxi, 12, 16–17, 106, 131

Heidegger, M., 115
Heraclitean universe, 92, 93
hermeneutics of predication, 7
heuristic discourse, 44, 45
historicity, xvi, xviii
history, xvii, 3
　of the universe, 47, 48
Hofmannsthal, H. v., 90
Hölderlin, F., 117

ideal of pure reason, 56, 113–14; *see also* sum total of all possibility
idealism, 80
　aesthetic, 15–16, 19
　analytic, 5
　semantic, 8, 10n12
　subjective, 18
　see also transcendental ideal
identity, xxix, 26, 126, 134–5
identity formula (world formula), 103–8
identity relation, 102
identity theory, 126–7
　of judgement, 126, 127–37
　of predication, 75–7, 78
indiscrete ontology, xx, 42
inductive inference, 40–1
inner-worldly dualism, 51
inner-worldly monism, 51, 52
intelligibility, 138–9
Intuition and Cognition (Hogrebe), xix
iteration *see* predicative rotation, theory of

James (3:6), 88
judgement, identity theory of, 126, 127–37
judgements *see Fa*-judgements

Kant and the Problem of Transcendental Semantics (Hogrebe), xiv, xix
Kant, I., 6, 18
　Critique of Pure Reason (CPR), xii, 53

ideal of pure reason, 56, 113–14, 116
metaphysics, 123–4
moral philosophy, 15–16
synthetic *a priori*, xv
transcendental deduction, xxix–xxx
transcendental ideal, 28–9, 52–8: Schelling's engagement with, 58–62 (*see also* theory of predicative elementary particles)
knowing, 15–16
knowledge, xxxi, 42–3
　of the past, xiv–xv
　proposition concerning the conservation of knowledge of beginnings, 73–4
　and self-organisation, 98–9
　of the world, 18, 39
　see also auto-epistemic structure of world / universe; epistemology; *Mitwissenschaft*
Krell, D.F., ix

language, 25, 40
　analytic philosophy of, 37, 43, 44
　see also pre-linguistic competence
Lebenskunst (Schelling), 22
limitation, mechanical explanation of, 60
logic, x, xii, 76
logical properties, 131
love, 26–7, 34n69, 79, 138
Löwenheim-Skolem theorem, 41
Lucinde (Schlegel), 11

madness, 26, 96, 97, 105, 109–11, 114, 116
meaning of being, xv, xvi, 8, 112–13
meaninglessness of being, xii–xiii, 8, 62
mechanical explanation of limitation, 60
memory *see* recollections
metaphysical properties, 131
metaphysics, viii, x–xi, xxix, 7, 8, 123–5, 137

and adequate conditions of
predication, 42–5
and conditions of successful
predication, 37–42
and existential conditions of
predication, 46–52
see also protophysics
Metaphysics and Mantics (Hogrebe),
xix, xx
Mitwissenschaft, xiv, xviii, 73–4, 79;
see also consciousness
monism, xxvi, 50, 51, 52, 123, 137
moral philosophy, 15–16
Myth of the Twentieth Century, The
(Rosenberg), 16, 31n29
mythical philosophy, 14
mythology, xiv, 80
new, 14–17, 21, 123: poetic
version, 21–4
mythos, 80

nature, xxx–xxxi, 14
nature-philosophy, 12, 17–19, 22, 25
nature's longing, 100
negation *see* original negation and
original affirmation
negative philosophy, 80
new mythology, 14–17, 21, 123
poetic version, 21–4
Nietzsche, F., 109

*Oldest System Programme of German
Idealism* (author uncertain), 15, 16, 23
'On Dante in Relation to Philosophy'
(Schelling), 12, 13, 20, 21
'On Kant's Ideal of Pure Reason'
(Schelling), 29, 68–9
On the Deities of Samothrace
(Schelling), 69, 80
*On the Myths, Historical Dicta and
Philosophemes of the Most Ancient
World* (Schelling), 14, 15
*On the Relationship of the Plastic Arts
to Nature* (Schelling), 22

'On the Source of Eternal Truths'
(Schelling), 69
ontology
discrete, 41, 43, 55
indiscrete, xx, 42
transcendental, 136–7
original negation and original
affirmation, 77–87
orphic reference, xi–xii, 66
outer-worldly dualism, 51–2

Parmenidean universe, 93
participant epistemology, xv
participant rationality, xiv
past, xiv–xv, 3–4
Patzig, G., 50
philosophy
analytic philosophy of language, 37, 43, 44
discourse-analytic potential, 5–6
discourse-creating potential, 6
moral, 15–16
mythical, 14
of mythology, 80
negative v. positive, 80, 114
and poesy, 17, 22–3, 32n21
transcendental, xvii–xviii, xxx
see also nature-philosophy
Philosophy of Art, The (Schelling), 12, 13, 19, 20, 27
Philosophy of Mythology (Schelling), xiv, 29
Philosophy of Revelation (Schelling), 113
'Physics as Art' (Ritter), xvi
Plato, xxiv, 12, 92, 116, 124
poesy, 17, 22–3, 32n21
poiesis, xviii
positive philosophy, 80, 114
possibility, sum total of, 55–6, 59–60, 113
possible, concept of, 59
potencies *see* theory of beginning
potentials
pre-linguistic competence, 38, 39
pre-linguistic level, 41

predicate logic, x, xii
predicates, 84
  Universal Register of, 53–5
predication, xii, 28
  adequate conditions of, 42–5
  conditions of successful, 37–42
  existential conditions of, 46–52
  hermeneutics of, 7
  identity theory of, 75–7, 78
  and Kant's theory of transcendental ideal, 52–8: Schelling's engagement with, 58–62 (*see also* predicative elementary particles, theory of)
  and love, 138
  principle of the initial conditions of, 53
predicative being, 63, 64, 65
  from chaos to order, 93, 95
  original negation and original affirmation, 78, 79, 80–1, 82, 84–5
  self-organisation, 99, 100
predicative elementary particles, theory of, 63–9
predicative rotation, theory of, 87–92, 94, 100
predicative space, 95
predicative time, 95
primal modality, 60, 61, 62
primordial being, 79, 80
primordial explosion, 81–2
principle of continuous determination, 53
principle of determinability, 53
Principle of Sufficient Reason, xii, xiii, xvi
principle of the further determination of predicates, 53
principle of the initial conditions of predication, 53
pronominal being, xi, 63–4, 65, 67, 128, 130
  from chaos to order, 93, 95, 96
  original negation and original affirmation, 78–9, 80–1, 82, 84, 85
  self-organisation, 99, 100
  world formula, 105
pronominal difference, 96–7
pronominal metaphysics, 124
proposition concerning the conservation of knowledge of beginnings, 73–4
propositional being, 65, 67, 82, 94, 95, 99
propositional variable, 95–6
protodynamics, theory of, 83–7
protophysics, 74

quiddative being *see* predicative being
Quine, W.V.O., 41, 42, 44
quoddative being *see* pronominal being

rationality, 122–3; *see also* participant rationality
reason, xii, xiii–xiv, xvii, 109–10, 113–15, 122; *see also* ideal of pure reason
recollections, 38–9, 40
reduplication of the copula, 128–9
reflections, 39
regress of judgement, 129, 131
repetition *see* predicative rotation, theory of
Ritter, J.W., xvi, xviii
Roddeweg, M., 13, 33n53
Rosenberg, A., 16, 31n29
Russell, B., 130
Ryle, G., 114–15

Schelling, F.W.J.
  as analytic idealist, 5
  engagement with Kant's transcendental ideal, 58–62: theory of predicative elementary particles, 63–9
  fundamental thought, xxix–xxx
  insignia, *1*

interest in Dante, 19–21
interpretation of Dante, 11–14, 24–8
on the past, 4
Schiller, F., xxxi–xxxii
Schlegel, C., 11, 12
Schlegel, F., 11–12, 20
Schröter, M., 27, 33n53
Science of Knowledge (Fichte), xxx
self-consciousness, xxiv, xxx, 103
self-construction, xx
self-identity, xxix–xxx
self-knowledge *see* auto-epistemic structure of world / universe
self-organisation, 97–102
and madness, 110
and world formula, 104, 105, 106, 107, 108
semantic idealism, 8, 10n12
singular judgements (*Fa*), 37, 40–1, 43, 49, 63, 70n14, 75–6
singular terms, 37–8, 39
soul-like essence, 99
space, 95–6
Space of Literature, The (Blanchot), xi
spirit, 95, 107–8, 138
start potential, 82, 83–4, 85
Strawson, P.F., 42
strict identity, 127
structure potential, 82, 85–7
subjective idealism, 18
sum total of all possibility, 55–6, 59–60, 113
sum total of all predicates, 53
synthetic *a priori*, xv, 48
System of Transcendental Idealism (Schelling), 12–13, 15, 17, 19, 23, 25

Tarski, A., xiii
theory of beginning potentials, 82–7
theory of predicative elementary particles, 63–9
theory of predicative rotation, 87–92, 94, 100
theory of protodynamics, 83–7
Third, 64–5
Timaeus (Plato), xxiv
time, 95–6, 106
To the Beloved (Schelling), 34n69
Tractatus logico-philosophicus (Wittgenstein), 126
transcendental affirmation, 57
transcendental deduction, xxix
transcendental ideal, 28–9, 52–8, 114
Schelling's engagement with, 58–62
transcendental metaphysics, 42
transcendental myth, 14
transcendental ontology, 136–7
Transcendental Ontology (Gabriel), xxxi
transcendental philosophy, xvii–xviii, xxx
truth conditions, 37, 50
truth theorem, Tarski, xiii
Tugendhat, E., 42

unity, 99–100, 106, 107, 133
Universal Register of predicates, 53–5
universal subject, 47
universe *see* world / universe

validity, 49, 50, 104
equal validity, 130
validity claims, 112
validity relations, xxxii
verification, 66

Weltgeheimnis (Hofmannsthal), 90
Wesen (essence), 44–5
will, 100–1
Wittgenstein, L., 37, 65, 126, 133
Wittgensteinian-Schelling Argument, 46
world / universe, 82, 88–9
auto-epistemic structure, x, xx, 46–8, 49, 51, 73, 107, 123

world / universe (*cont.*)
  genesis, 60–2, 63, 107–8
  Heraclitean universe, 92, 93
  Parmenidean universe, 93
  see also cosmic inconsistency

World Catalogue (Hasenjaeger), 54
world formula, 103–8
Worldsoul, The (Schelling), 12, 47

Zeno, E., xiv, xvi